MESSIANIC CODE OF JEWISH LAW

RAY LOOKER

Messianic Code of Jewish Law

Author: Ray Looker

All Scriptures are from the King James Bible

ISBN-13:978-1481850179

   -10:1481850172

Think not that I am come to destroy the Law, or the prophets: I am not come to destroy, but to fulfill. For verily I say unto you, Till heaven and earth pass, one jot or one title shall in no wise pass from the law till all be fulfilled.

Whosoever therefore shall break one of these least commandments, and shall teach men so, he shall be called the least in the Kingdom of Heaven; but whosoever shall do and teach them the same shall be called great in the Kingdom of Heaven.

(Matthew 5:17-19)

Dedicated to My Beloved Wife Chianna

My Friends Rev. & Mrs. Robert Manning

And

The Honorable & Mrs. John-Bob Woofter

(CSMAJ, U.S. Army – Retired)

PROLOGUE

The enclosed "Messianic Code of Jewish Law", is an adaptation of those aspects of Jewish Law which every believer should know and do. Each law is based upon a Biblical Mandate, and each precept is based upon how to observe that Mandate. Under the Messianic Covenant we have an enhancement of the concept of law administered in love. The love of a father with a child expresses a new concept of legal administration not previously in evidence, but is expressed more specifically in the Messianic Covenant:

"Charity suffers long, and is kind: Charity envies not itself, is not puffed up does not behave itself unseemly, seeks not her own, is not easily provoked, thinks no evil. Rejoices not in iniquity, but rejoices in the truth; bears all things, hopes all things, endures all things, charity never fails."

Our obedience to Yahweh our Father is not based upon our fear of reprisal, although that is always present; it is based upon a desire to please Him who has died for us. The Law is our schoolmaster which teaches us how to please Yahweh.

Inherit in pleasing Yahweh, is how we treat others. Even as Yahweh, on a rather frequent basis, is asked to forgive us our sins, even so He is pleased when we forgive others. As Yahweh has forgiven us by His mercy, for the wages of sin is death, even so must we be merciful and forgive others. Mercy is the balance of righteousness in judgment.

We have presented the following "Code" as a guide to the administration of Jewish Law based upon Holy Scripture and the Messianic Covenant. There is surely a reconciliation of the two as the one is an extension of the other. While the Feasts of Yahweh are mandated in Scripture, the details of how they are observed has not been specified, nor taught within Christianity. The Jewish Code for their observances is presented only as a guide to their observance.

Other observances, such as the use of the Mezuzah, Tefillin, and Tallit, are all based upon a

Biblical Mandate, of which we have only the Jewish example to guide us. The apostle Paul in speaking to the Romans, 3:2; said that it was unto the Jews that the Oracles of Yahweh were committed. Such an acknowledgment lends creditability to our claim that Jewish examples of observances are a valid source of guidance in how to keep a particular Mandate. It is evident that Gentile Christian Churches have been remiss in providing that instruction.

In preparing the Bride for the coming of Yahshua the Messiah, this Messianic Code of Jewish Law seeks to educate all Believers on the Laws of Yahweh and perhaps instill a desire to keep them in preparation for the day when we will be called upon to administer them in the Kingdom of our Lord.

Since the First Century (Common Era), when the Gentile Nicolaitan Church broke away from the Counsel of Jerusalem and the Doctrine of the Apostles, Gentile Believers have been taught that they are no longer under the Law of Yahweh. These rebellious Nicolaitan Churches established their own religious sect, somewhat based upon the Gospel, and more so on the assimilation of various pagan Babylonian religious practices. They instituted a new set of laws, separate from those established by the Word of Yahweh in Scripture, i.e., the written Torah. This has resulted in a "catechism" of over two thousand eight hundred precepts. None of which should be of any interest to the Believer. We are not called to keep the laws and customs of the heathen, for the ways of the heathen are vain. See Jeremiah 10:2-3.

By assimilating the doctrines and traditions of Babylon, the Gentile Church has made the Word of Yahweh of non-effect. That is, they have made void the Word of Yahweh by their traditions. Yahshua gives us warning in Matthew 15:3, 6, 9; and Mark 7:7-9, and 13; and such as these: in Psalm 119:126 and 136:

> "It is time for Thee Lord to work: for they have made void the Law."

> "Rivers of waters run down mine eyes, because they keep not Your Law."

The argument has been presented that we are no longer under the Law, because we are under Grace, is only valid if, indeed, we are truly in Yahweh. One cannot be "in Yahweh" and yet continue to sin. One cannot be "in Yahweh" and not keep His Commandments. To be "in Yahweh," we are truly beyond the reach of the Law; we have not sinned, nor do we sin, because we do not transgress the Laws of Yahweh, contrary, we uphold the Law by our actions.

A society that has no laws is a lawless society. It is inconceivable that after Messiah Yahshua came, all the Laws of Yahweh were suspended until His return to set up His Kingdom on earth; a "Kingdom" which will be ruled with a Rod of Iron, i.e., the Law, the written Torah, the Holy Word of Yahweh. And if the written Torah shall be administered during Messiah's reign, then how much more will the application of that same Law apply to us today.

In Preparing the Bride for the coming Deliverer, the call of Yahweh is for the restoration of the Church upon its original foundation of Judeo-Christianity. To do this we must once more establish the Law of Yahweh as the foundation upon which that restoration is premised, and the Feasts of Yahweh which provides the structure for building the Temple of Yahweh within our lives.

Christian Holidays of Advent, Christmas, Lent, Easter, and Halloween, are not a part of this study because they are not of the Christian religion. They are not in Scripture, and therefore, we must conclude, they are not Christian in nature or in scope. Sunday Worship, falsely called the "Christian Sabbath," is a lying fraud. Its sole purpose is to render honor to the authority of the Catholic churches, in honor of the Sun-god. The First day of the week is celebrated to acknowledge Satan's desired position as number one in the universe.

The following study on the Messianic Code of Jewish Law, is an attempt to syncretize Judeo-Christianity as a viable step in the Church's responsibility to prepare herself for the coming of Yahweh, and to teach Gentile Believers the Laws of Yahweh, wherewith they will sit as kings and priests to judge the nations during the thousand year reign of the Messiah.

To achieve syncretism, there must first come an understanding. While many traditions of the Jewish law are foreign to Gentile Believers, and we will not even attempt to explore, or present the full depth of those traditions, we do present a clearer dialogue of those, which, we feel, Believing Jews should continue to observe, and to which even Gentile Believers might aspire in the keeping of them. These particular beliefs and traditions are the result of Jewish attempts to keep particular Commandments of Yahweh. Lacking any other example from which we can draw upon, they are presented, hopefully, without any attempt to exact more than what the Commandment requires.

The prophet Micah (6:8), states that what Yahweh requires of us is "to do justly, to love mercy, and to walk humbly with your God."

Zechariah (7:9-10), says that Yahweh expects us to:

> "Execute true justice, show mercy and compassion, everyone to his brother. Do not oppress the widow, or the fatherless, the alien, or the poor. Let none of you plan evil in his heart against his brother."

Yahshua, the Messiah, has reminded us in Matthew 23:23; that the weightier matters of the Law are: Justice, Mercy, and Faith.

Solomon, in Ecclesiastes 12:13-14, states:

"Fear Yahweh and keep His Commandments, for this is the whole duty of man. For Yahweh shall bring every work into judgment, with every secret thing, whether it be good, or whether it be evil."

Do we fear Yahweh? Do we keep His Commandments?   Yahshua has said in John 14:15:

"If you love me, you will keep my commandments."

And again in John 15:10 Yahshua says:

If you keep my commandments you shall abide in my love; even as I have kept my Father's Commandments, and abide in His Love."

In I John 5:2-3, it states:

"By this we know that we love the children of Yahweh, when we love Yahweh, and keep His Commandments. This is the Love of Yahweh that we keep His Commandments, and His Commandments are not grievous."

In Matthew 11:28-30, Yahshua says:

> "Come unto me, all you that labour and are
> heavy laden and I will give you rest. Take my
> yoke upon you, and learn of me; for I am
> meek and lowly in heart, and you shall find
> rest for your souls. For my yoke is easy, and
> my burden is light."

Anyone who says that we must not keep the
Commandments of Yahweh, because we are under
Grace, is a liar, and the truth is not in him. Messiah
Yahshua says that those who keep the Law, and
teach others to keep the Law shall be called great in
the Kingdom of Heaven. (Matthew 5:19). In a letter
to the Romans, the apostle Paul in Romans 2:12-13,
states:

> "For as many as have sinned without the Law
> shall also perish without law; and as many as
> have sinned in the Law shall be judged by the
> Law; for not the hearts of Law are just before
> Yahweh, but the doers of the Law shall be
> justified."

The apostle Paul goes on in Romans 7:12, and
states:

> "Wherefore the Law is Holy, and the
> Commandment Holy, and Just and Good."

King David in Psalm 19 declares:

"The Law of Yahweh is perfect, converting the soul the testimony of Yahweh is sure, making wise the simple, the Statutes of Yahweh are right, rejoicing the heart; the Commandment of Yahweh is pure, enlightening the eyes. The Fear of Yahweh is clean, enduring forever. The Judgments of Yahweh are true and righteous all together. More to be desired are they than gold, yea, than much fine gold: Sweeter also than honey and the honeycomb. Moreover by them is your servant warned: and in keeping them there is great reward.

Psalm 119 has 176 verses in praise of the Law of Yahweh. The Law of Yahweh is a Lamp unto our feet, and a Light unto our path. Wherewithal a young man shall cleanse his way is by taking heed thereto according to the Law.

This Messianic Code of Jewish Law differs in construct from the four-volume Code of Jewish Law, in that it covers not only major aspects of the Jewish Law, but it also incorporates major aspects of the Messianic Code.

Yahweh's covenant agreement with His people has been stated and restated in Scripture to Abraham, Isaac, Jacob, and to Moses and the Prophets. When the Law was given to Moses at Mount Sinai, a tenet of Jewish tradition is that as individuals we must see ourselves as having personally gone forth from Egypt and stood at Mount Sinai, and the Law (the written Torah) was in fact given to us and not to our forefathers alone, so that we are ever involved in the renewal of our personal commitment to it.

This moral obligation stems from our personal consent and agreement to become a partner with Yahweh in the administration of that Law. Gentile Believers who have been baptized in the Name of Yahshua have been grafted into the Judaic vine, and have likewise, through the Law of Adoption, become responsible to keep the Laws of Yahweh, and to teach their children as well.

A principle which must be understood in a covenant agreement is that legally each of the parties to the agreement is required to observe the dictates of the covenant agreement. While the Believer is required to keep the Laws of Yahweh, the premise is always stated that if we will keep Yahweh's Commandments, He will pour out His

Blessings upon us. He will protect us and keep us from all harm; He will expand our borders, He will keep in perfect peace those who trust in His Word, and obey His Commandments. This is well stated in Deuteronomy 28:1-14, and again in the giving of the Tithe in Malachi 3:10-11:

> "Bring all the Tithes into the storehouse, that there may be meat in mine house, and prove me now herewith, says Yahweh, Lord of Hosts, if I will not open you the windows of heaven, and pour you out a Blessing, that there shall not be room enough to receive it. And I will rebuke the devourer for your sakes."

Clearly, a covenant is not one sided. Yahweh is also bound by the covenant, and is deeply committed to it. So deeply is Yahweh committed to the covenant that He sent His only begotten Son as the principal mediator of the Law, having fulfilled in His own flesh the dictates of the Law so that even Gentiles receive the Blessings of Yahweh through obedience to the Law. Believers have entered into the covenant relationship with Yahweh through faith in the salvation which can only come through the shed Blood of Yahshua the Messiah, and in obedience to His Word, been baptized in the Name of Yahshua.

Keeping the Law and receiving the circumcision in the flesh is no guarantee that anyone is saved. The Law specifically requires a circumcision of the heart, a shedding of Blood, and the passing through the Waters of Purification and Separation which can only be done under the Messianic Covenant. Yahshua achieved this on our behalf when He offered Himself as a one-time sacrifice for all time.

Baptism is more than just a public statement of belief it is the first act of obedience which spiritually cleanses and separates the Believer unto Yahweh. The shed Blood of Yahshua was appropriated in fulfillment of the Law which states that without the shedding of Blood there is no remission of sin, as stated in Leviticus 17:11.

This is a Jewish Law, commanded by Yahweh, which applies to all, Jew and Gentile. Anyone, Jew or Gentile who enters the Tabernacle of Yahweh without first passing through the Waters of Purification and Separation has defiled the

Tabernacle of Yahweh. See Numbers, Chapter 19 on the Ashes of the Red Heifer, and the Waters of Purification and Separation.

Having been baptized and passed through the Waters of Separation and Purification in obedience to His Word, we can come boldly unto the Throne of Grace, the Mercy Seat, that we may obtain mercy, and find grace to help in time of need. See Hebrews 4:16.

Once an individual has entered into a Covenant relationship with Yahweh, there is an obligation to follow the teachings of the Law, so that we might more accurately reflect the Kingdom of Yahweh in our lives. Yahweh will do what we ask of Him, because we do those things which are pleasing to Him, if not for our sakes, at least for His Name's sake He will do it. We can only know what He wants us to do by learning the Law and applying the precepts of the Law in our lives. As the Prophet Samuel said to King Saul in I Samuel 15:22:

"To obey is better than sacrifice, and to hearken than the fat of rams."

The Law was given to teach us the way of righteousness. It is a lamp unto our feet. It is also the media by which we will judge the nations when Messiah comes.

While some laws are rather clear in how they must be observed, others are unclear. The implication is that we can adapt such to our own understanding. In many cases Judaism has taken a more literal position and proscribed only one way. While perhaps not entirely correct, it does provide a valid example from which we can seek guidance, since there is no other example to draw from.

In the administration of Law we must never forget to apply the concept of mercy to others, which Yahweh has so freely applied to our own personal sins. The commandment to love one another, which Yahshua gives carries with it the admonition to forgive one another even as He has forgiven us.

In a letter to the Churches, the Council of Jerusalem was in agreement that the Gentile believers would not be held to the same standard as were the Jews. The demand was that they were to "abstain from pollutions of idols, and from fornication, and from things strangled, and from Blood." (See Acts 15:20).

These four things, Idolatry, Fornication, Strangled meat, and the eating and drinking of Blood, included the observance of pagan rituals and animal sacrifices to false gods. All of which is present in the Church today. Since the Ministers can no longer distinguish between the Holy and the profane, Yahweh's Name is profaned among the nations. Spiritual fornication is a sin against the temple of Yahweh, and the Holy Spirit which dwells within.

In Christian communities around the world we find the eating of blood cakes, and even the drinking of blood practiced as part of the cultural heritage of the people. Even the eating of rare meat in modern cultures contains a goodly amount of blood, which the Church, in spite of the fact that both the Hebrew Scriptures and the Messianic Covenant strongly speak against the eating or the drinking of blood.

The focus of this book will be principally on those Laws which Yahweh Himself commanded. It is then up to the Jewish and Christian Believer as to how they choose to obey those Laws, but obey they must, if they choose to please Yahweh.

To My Beloved Chi-Anna, to Reverend and Mrs. Robert Manning, and to the Honorable and Mrs. John-Bob Woofter, I dedicate this book. They and they alone stood beside me and encouraged me when all others fled. The Grace of Yahweh and Yahshua the Messiah be with you and Bless you as you seek to do those things which are pleasing to Him.

Ray Looker - Tevet 5764 (2004)

CONTENTS

PART II DIETARY LAWS

PART III   THE MORAL LAWS

PART IV   FESTIVALS

They (the priests) shall teach my people the difference between the Holy and profane, and cause them to discern between the unclean and the clean.

And in controversy they shall stand in judgment, and they shall judge it according to my judgments, and they shall keep my Laws and my statutes in all mine assemblies, and they shall hallow my Sabbaths.

(Ezekiel 44:23-24)

INTRODUCTION

In the beginning, when Yahweh created the heavens and the earth, and all that was in it in six days, He created each animal, fish, fowl, and creeping things after his own kind. This means that Yahweh did not create the heavens and the earth and all that was in it in five billion years. Yahweh created all things in six literal days, even as the Scripture says.

The Scripture does not say that each animal evolved from a single-cell life form, and as each cell formed it adapted to the environment in which it found itself. Nor does the Scripture say that each cell found a variety of methods of evolving into different life forms, while keeping similar genetic traits such as eyes, ears, skin, hair, fur, scales and feathers; and different forms of mobility such as two-legs, four legs, wings and fins.

Mankind's adaptation to the environment was not biological, it was mechanical. We adapted with clothing, cars, scooters, airplanes, scuba gear, etc. Our superior intelligence has never allowed us to adapt through biological adaptation such as the evolutionists would have us believe occurred over the course of five billion years for other life forms.

Each life form was created to be capable of homeostasis within the environment in which it was placed by its Creator. Even though all life forms were created from common elements in the earth, each was created, and reproduced after his own kind. Meaning, of course, that the Creator of each life form set a barrier in the genetic code which prevented cross fertilization between the species.

Only in mythology do we find any semblance of cross fertilization, i.e., a man with goat's feet, or with the lower body of a horse, or a mermaid having a female upper body and a lower body of a fish with a tail. If evolution were valid, then we would see a digression to similarity of all species.

Even in the plant kingdom we see this same barrier to cross fertilization. Within a species we can do some amazing experiments, yet beyond the species we can do nothing.

On the sixth day Yahweh created man in His image and gave him dominion over all His creation, and on the seventh day Yahweh rested. It is said that on the seventh day Yahweh created a Sabbath rest. He separated the seventh day from the first six days of creation, blessed it, and sanctified it above all other days.

In Judaism, as well as in Christianity, Yahweh is a given. He is and has always been, and He is the Creator of the universe and all that is in it. This concept of Yahweh is the foundation of our faith. To keep the Sabbath, the seventh day, as a day of rest, both spiritual and physical, is to observe the first of Yahweh's festivals, and is a covenant sign which bears witness to our belief that in sixth days Yahweh created the heavens and the earth.

To desecrate the Sabbath is to profane the name of Yahweh, but to keep His Commandments and His Statutes as found in the written Torah, the Law of Yahweh, the Word of Yahweh, is the desire of Yahweh.

When Yahweh placed Adam and Eve in the Garden of Eden, they were instructed not to eat of the Tree of the Knowledge of Good and Evil, for in the day that they should eat of it they would surely die. The serpent, the devil, Satan, with cunning and with deceit convinced Eve to eat the fruit of the tree of the knowledge of good and evil. Taking the fruit offered to her," Eve ate it and gave it to Adam, and he ate of it also. Seeing that they were naked they sewed fig leaves together, made themselves aprons, and hid from Yahweh when they heard His voice walking in the Garden.

The outcome of this original sin was expulsion from the Garden of Eden, and a variety of curses upon the man, the woman, the serpent, Satan, and upon the ground. Until the fall of Adam, there was no death in the universe recorded in Scripture.

When Adam fell from grace, then death entered the universe and the second law of thermodynamics was instituted. When Yahweh drove Adam and Eve from the Garden of Eden, He made coats of skins and clothed them. Herein lies another point: Adam and Eve used fig leaves to make an apron, while Yahweh used skins of animals to make coats for them. The fig leaves were not sufficient to convey the concept of death which the outcome of sin causes, nor did fig leaves provide the necessary covering. The coats of animal skins did fulfill the law of death and the shedding of blood required for atonement.

Later we see that when Cain and Abel made their sacrifices to Yahweh, Cain's offering was not accepted because, like the fig leaves, it did not atone for sin. In Leviticus 17:11, Yahweh says that it is the blood which makes atonement for the soul. In Hebrews 9:22, Yahweh again says that without the shedding of blood there is no remission of sin. Today the Rabbi's say that atonement is made through repentance, prayer, and doing good deeds. This does not fulfill the requirement for the shedding of blood for the remission of sin. So, how does one fulfill the requirement of the Law so that their sins may receive atonement, since the Temple and animal sacrifices are no longer available? Yahweh has provided a way so that every sin can receive atonement. This applies to the Jew as well as the Christian Believer.

When Yahweh cursed the serpent, Satan, He put enmity between Satan and the woman and between Satan's seed, the children of the world, and her seed, which is the Messiah, who will bruise Satan's head, and Satan will bruise His heel. When Yahshua offered Himself on the altar of sacrifice, He fulfilled the requirement of the Law, and offered

Himself as a one-time sacrifice for all time. As the Messiah, and High Priest of Yahweh after the order of Melchizedek, He offered Himself and shed His blood for our sins. Today we don't need the sacrifice of bulls and goats to atone for our sins, but we do need to appropriate the sacrifice of blood which was provided through His Son, Yahshua the Messiah.

When Abraham bound Isaac upon the altar, Yahweh gave him a substitutionary offering, the ram caught in the bush. Conversely, we see that Yahweh did offer His Son as a sacrifice, a substitutionary offering for our sins. While this sacrifice is available, it is only available to those who believe in His name and appropriate His blood sacrifice for our sins. Yahshua the Messiah by His own blood entered into the Holy of Holies, through the veil of His flesh, having obtained eternal redemption for us. For this cause Yahshua is the mediator of the New Covenant for both Jew and Gentile alike. (Hebrews, Chapter 9).

The Scriptures clearly reveal in both the Hebrew Scriptures and the Messianic Covenant that mankind continues to commit sins, whether willingly or unwillingly, knowingly or unknowingly, in ignorance as well as in knowledge.

For all have sinned and come short of the Glory of Yahweh. And there are none righteous, no not one. If anyone says that he has not sinned, he is a liar and the truth is not in him. These are all recorded in the Epistle of I John, Chapter 1, which also says that if we confess our sins, He is faithful and just to forgive us our sins and to cleanse us from all unrighteousness. Chapter 3, of I John goes on to state that if we do sin, we have an advocate with the Father, Yahshua the Messiah, the Righteous One.

Prior to Yahshua's sacrifice and resurrection, only Jews were considered the children of Yahweh, because only the Jews kept the Law of Yahweh and worshipped the Creator of all life. However, after the sacrifice, resurrection and ascension of Yahshua into heaven, the door to salvation was opened to the Gentiles as well as to the Jew. In Ephesians, Chapter 2, the Scripture indicates that where once the Gentile was without hope, that through the veil of the flesh of Yahshua the Messiah, and His shed blood, Yahshua has broken down the wall of partition which separated Gentile and Jew, and made them one, so that He could reconcile both to Yahweh in one body by His sacrifice on the altar.

The apostle Paul, in writing to the Ephesians, Chapter 2, continues to assert that Gentiles are fellow citizens with the saints, and are of the household of Yahweh. He further states that they are built upon the foundation of the apostles and prophets, which is the written Torah, of which Yahshua is the chief corner stone. Yahshua is the chief corner stone of the Torah, the Law of Yahweh, because He, the Messiah, is the fulfillment of the Law. It is clear that Gentiles were grafted into the Judaic vine.

Nowhere in Scripture does it say that Gentiles were grafted into the Babylonian vine. Contrary, the Scriptures are clear in stating that they were cut from a wild vine and grafted into a goodly vine, Yahshua said," I am the vine, you are the branches." If we continue to abide in Him then we will bear much fruit. The root of Christianity is Judaism. To be severed from the root is to become grafted into a wild vine, the vine of Babylon, the Synagogue of Satan.

To raise up the Tabernacle of David, to rebuild the walls of Jerusalem, the Church must prepare herself for the coming of Yahweh by returning to the Laws which were commanded by and constitute the foundation of our faith. Like Nehemiah and Ezra, we too must sever ourselves from all pagan practices and once more reestablish the foundation of the Law in our lives and in our Churches. It is only as we return that we once more make Holy the name of Yahweh. It is only as we repent and return that we truly lift up the name of Yahshua among the nations. How can we make the Jewish people jealous of our fellowship with Yahweh? This is done only by keeping the Commandments and Statutes of Yahweh more perfectly. But this can only be done through joy, peace, love and mercy. As we administer Yahweh's Law in the Love of Yahshua, we surpass even the intent of the Law.

PART I

The Commandments of Yahweh

Shema Israel Adonai elohaynu Adonai echad.
Baruch Shaym K'vod Mal'chuso L'olam Vaed.

[Hear O Israel, Yahweh is our God, Yahweh is one,
Blessed is His name and His glorious Kingdom
forever and ever.]

Chapter 1

You shall have no other gods before me.

(Exodus 20:3 and Deuteronomy 5:7)

§1.1 Deuteronomy 6:5   You shall love Yahweh your God with all your heart, and with all your soul and with all your might. (See also Matthew 22:36)

§1.2 Matthew 4:10   You shall worship Yahweh your God, and Him only shall you serve.

§1.3 Deuteronomy 6:13   You shall fear Yahweh your God, and serve Him, and shall swear by His name.

§1.4 <u>Deuteronomy 6:14-15</u>   You shall not go after other gods, of the gods of the people which are round about you; for Yahweh your God is a jealous God among you.

§1 .5 <u>Hebrews 11:6</u>   Without faith it is impossible to please Him. For he that comes to Yahweh must believe that He is, and that He is a rewarder of them that diligently seek Him.

§1.6 <u>Isaiah 6:3</u>   Holy, Holy, Holy, is Yahweh, Lord of hosts. The whole earth is full of His glory.

§1.7 <u>Revelation 4:8</u>   Holy, Holy, Holy, is Yahweh, Lord God Almighty, which was, and is, and is to come.

§1.8 <u>Isaiah 41:4</u>   I Yahweh, the first and with the last, I am He. (Isaiah 44:8; 45:5, 45:18; 46:9, 48:12).

§1.9 <u>Revelation 1:11</u>   I am Alpha and Omega, the first and the last.

§1.10 <u>Revelation 22:13</u>   I am Alpha and Omega, the beginning and the end, the first and the last.

§1.11 <u>James 2:19</u>   You believe that there is one God, you do well, the devils also believe, and tremble.

§1:12 <u>Deuteronomy 6:16</u>   You shall not tempt Yahweh your God, as you tempted Him in Massah.

§1.13 <u>Deuteronomy 6:17</u>   You shall diligently keep the commandments of Yahweh your God, and His testimonies, and His statutes, which He has commanded you.

§1.14 <u>Deuteronomy 6:18</u>   And you shall do that which is right and good in the sight of Yahweh, that it may be well with you, and that you may go in and possess the good land which Yahweh swore unto your fathers.

§1.15 <u>Isaiah 44:6</u>   Thus saith Yahweh, the King of Israel, and His Redeemer the Lord of Hosts, I am the first, and I am the last, and beside me there is no God.

§1.16 <u>Isaiah 43:10-11</u>   I am He, before me there was no God, neither shall there be after me. I, even I, am Yahweh, and beside me there is no Savior.

§1.17 <u>John 14:1-3</u>   Let not your heart be troubled, you believe in Yahweh, believe also in me. In my Father's house are many mansions, if it were not so, I would have told you, I go to prepare a place for you. And if I go to prepare a place for you, I will come again, and receive you unto myself, that where I am, there you may be also.

§1.18 <u>John 14:6-7</u>   Yahshua said, "I am the way, the truth, the life, no man comes to the Father, but by me.   If you had known me, you should have known my Father also, and henceforth you know Him, and have seen Him."

§1.19 <u>John 14:9</u>   Yahshua said to him, "Have I been so long time with you, and yet have you not known me, Phillip? He that has seen me has seen the Father."

Chapter 2

You shall not make unto you any graven image, or any likeness of anything that is in heaven above, or that is in the earth beneath, or that is in the water under the earth.

You shall not bow down yourself to them, nor serve them; for I Yahweh your God am a jealous God, visiting the iniquity of the fathers upon the children unto the third and fourth generations of them that hate me.

And showing mercy unto thousands of them that love me and keep my commandments.

(Exodus 20: 4/Deuteronomy 5:8)

§2.1 <u>Leviticus 19:4</u> Turn not unto idols, nor make yourselves molten gods.

§2:2 Psalm 135:15-18   The idols of the heathen are silver and gold, the work of men's hands. They have mouths, but they speak not, eyes have they, but they see not. They have ears, but they hear not. Neither is there any breath in their mouths. They that make them are like unto them. So is every one that trusts in them.

§2.3 Jeremiah 10:3   The customs of the people are vain, for one cuts a tree out of the forest, the work of the hands of the workmen, with the ax. They deck it with silver and with gold. They fasten it with nails and with hammers, that it move not. They are upright as the palm tree, but speak not they must needs be borne, because they cannot go. Be not afraid of them, for they cannot do evil, neither also is it in them to do good.

§2.4 Exodus 23:13   Make no mention of the name of other gods, neither let it be heard out of your mouth.

§2.5 It is forbidden to look at idols or to admire their ornaments. One must keep away from a house of idolatry, and especially from an idol.

§2.6 II Kings 18:4 Hezekiah broke in pieces the brazen serpent that Moses had made. For unto those days the children of Israel did burn incense to it, and he called it Nehush'tan (a bronze thing).

§2.7 The veneration of pictures, icons, rosaries, religious relics, and so-called sacred images is an abomination unto Yahweh.

§2.8 Exodus 30:31-33 This shall be a Holy anointing oil unto me throughout your generations. Upon man's flesh shall it not be poured, neither shall you make any other like it, after the composition of it. It is Holy, and it shall be Holy unto you. Whosoever compounds any like it, or whosoever puts any of it upon a stranger, shall even be cut off from his people.

§2.9 <u>Exodus 30:34-39</u>   Take you sweet spices ... and you shall make a perfume ... , tempered together, Pure and Holy... and put it before the Testimony in the Tabernacle of the Congregation, where I will meet with you, it shall be unto you most Holy ... you shall not make to yourselves according to the composition thereof . It shall be unto you Holy for Yahweh. Whosoever shall make like unto that, to smell thereto, shall even be cut off from his people.

§2.10 It is forbidden to prepare incense, or ointment oil in the same formula and in the same weight as proscribed in the Scriptures. However, if one prepares it only for the purpose of it, he is not guilty.

Chapter 3

You shall not take the name of Yahweh your God in vain for Yahweh will not hold him guiltless that takes His name in vain.

(Exodus 20:7 / Deuteronomy 5:11)

§3.1 Psalm 8:1   O Yahweh our Lord, how excellent is Your name in all the earth!

§3.2 Deuteronomy 6:13   You shall fear Yahweh your God, and serve Him, and shall swear by His name.

§3.3 Revelation 15:4   Who shall not fear You Yahweh and glorify Your name? For You are Holy; for all nations shall come and worship before You.

§3.4 <u>Proverbs 18:10</u>   The Name of Yahweh is a High Tower, the righteous run into it, and are safe.

§3.5 <u>Philippians 2:9-10</u>   Wherefore Yahweh also has highly exalted Him, and given Him a name which is above every name, that at the name of Yahshua, every knee shall bow and every tongue confess that Yahshua is Lord, to the glory of Yahweh the Father.

§3.6 <u>Isaiah 45:23</u>   I have sworn by myself, the Word is gone out of my mouth in righteousness, and shall not return, that unto me every knee shall bow and every tongue shall swear.

§3.7 <u>Acts 4:12</u>   Neither is there salvation in any other, for there is none other name under heaven given among men, whereby we must be saved.

§3.8 <u>John 14:13</u>   And whatever you shall ask in my Name, that will I do, that the

Father may be glorified in the Son. If you shall ask anything in my Name, I will do it.

§3.9 <u>Leviticus 19:12</u>   And you shall not swear by my Name falsely, neither shall you profane the name of Yahweh your God.

§3.10 <u>Deuteronomy 23:21-23</u>   When you shall vow a vow unto Yahweh your God, you shall not slack to pay it. For Yahweh your God will surely require it of you, and it would be sin to you. That which is gone out of your lips you shall keep and perform. Even a freewill offering, according as you hast vowed unto Yahweh your God which you has promised.

§3.11 <u>Matthew 5:33-37</u>   You have heard it has been said by them of old time, you shall not forswear yourself, but shall perform unto Yahweh your oaths. But I say unto you, Swear not at all, neither by heaven, for it is Yahweh's throne, nor by the earth, for it is His footstool, neither by Jerusalem, for it is the city of the great King. Neither shall you swear by your head, because you cannot make one hair white or black. But let your communication be, yea, yea, nay, nay, for whatsoever is more than these comes of evil. (James 5:12).

Chapter 4

Keep the Sabbath day to sanctify it, as Yahweh your God has commanded you. Six days you shall labour, and do your work, but the seventh day is the Sabbath of Yahweh your God.

In it you shall not do any work, you, nor your son, nor your daughter, nor your manservant, nor your maidservant, nor your ox, nor your ass, nor any of your cattle, nor your stranger that is within your gates; that your manservant and your maidservant may rest as well as you.

For in six days Yahweh made heaven and earth, the sea, and all that is in them, and rested the seventh day. Wherefore Yahweh blessed the seventh day, and hallowed it.

(Genesis 2:1-3; Exodus 20:8-11; Deuteronomy 5:12-15)

§4.1 <u>Exodus 31:13-17</u>   Verily my Sabbaths you shall keep for it is a sign between me and you throughout your generations. That you may know that I am Yahweh that does sanctify you. You shall keep the Sabbath therefore, for it is Holy unto you, everyone that defiles it shall surely be put to death. For whosoever does any work therein, that soul shall be cut off from among his people.

Six days may work be done, but in the seventh day is the Sabbath of rest, Holy to Yahweh. Whosoever does any work in the Sabbath day, he shall be put to death. Wherefore the children of Israel shall keep the Sabbath, to observe the Sabbath throughout their generations, for a perpetual covenant. It is a sign between me and the children of Israel forever. For in six days Yahweh made heaven and earth, and on the seventh day He rested, and was refreshed.

§4.2 <u>Leviticus 19:30 and 26:2</u>   You shall keep my Sabbaths, and reverence my Sanctuary.

§4.3 <u>Jeremiah 17:22</u>   Neither carry forth a burden out of your house on the Sabbath day, neither do you any work, but hallow you the Sabbath day, as I commanded your fathers.

§4.4 <u>Ezekiel 20:12 and 20:20</u>   Moreover also I gave them my Sabbaths, to be a sign between me and them, that they might know that I am Yahweh that sanctify them. And hallow your Sabbaths.

§4.5 <u>Matthew 12:8</u>   For the Son of Man is Lord even of the Sabbath day. (See also Mark 2:28 and Luke 6:5)

§4.6 <u>Matthew 12:22</u>   Wherefore it is lawful to do well on the Sabbath days.

Chapter 5

Honor your father and your mother; that your days may be long upon the land which Yahweh your God gives you.

(Exodus 20:12 / Deuteronomy 5:16)

§5.1 <u>Exodus 21:17</u>   He that curses his father, or his mother, shall surely be put to death. (See also Matthew 15:4 and Mark 7:10)

§5.2 <u>Deuteronomy 27:16</u>   Cursed be he that dishonors his father or his mother.

§5.3 <u>Leviticus 19:3</u>   You shall fear every man his mother, and his father, and you shall keep my Sabbaths.

§5.4 <u>Colossians 3:20</u>   Children obey your parents in all things, for this is well pleasing unto Yahweh. (See also Ephesians 6:1-2)

§5.5 One must provide father and mother with food and drink, clothing, and all their needs cheerfully. One must not occupy the place appointed for one's father. One must neither contradict, nor corroborate his father's words. He should never insult his parents nor show anger towards them, but he should remain silent and fear Yahweh who is the King of kings, and Lord of lords.

§5.6 Even if his father is wicked and a sinner, he must fear and revere him. Even an illegitimate child is bound to honor and fear his father.

§5.7 A child should not hearken to his father when he tells him to transgress a precept of the Scriptures. It is written that Yahweh is God and both the

28

children and the parents are equally bound to honor Yahweh.

§5.8 He who truly wishes to honor his father and his mother, should devote to the study of Scripture, and to the performance of good deeds for this is the greatest honor to his parents.

§5.9 Likewise, a father who is concerned about the welfare of his children, should also engage in the study of Scripture and the doing of good deeds, so that he may please his Father in Heaven and thus cause his children to be proud of him.

§5.10 A person must respect his step-mother during his father's lifetime and his stepfather during his mother's lifetime. And it is proper that one should honor stepparents even after the death of one's own parents.

§5.11 <u>Ephesians 6:4</u>   Fathers, provoke not your children to wrath, but bring them up in the nurture and admonition of Yahweh.

§5.12 A father is forbidden to place a burdensome yoke upon his children; he must not be too exacting in demanding honor from them, so that he may cause them to stumble into sin. He should rather overlook their short-comings and forgive them.

Chapter 6

You shall not kill.

(Exodus 20:13 / Deuteronomy 5:17)

§6.1 <u>Genesis 9:5</u>   And surely your blood of your lives will I require, at the hand of every beast will I require it, and at the hand of man, at the hand of every man's brother will I require the life of man. (To include suicide and abortion)

§6.2 <u>Genesis 9:6</u>   Whoever sheds man's blood, by man shall his blood be shed, for in the image of Yahweh made He man.

§6.3 <u>Exodus 21:12</u>   He that smites a man, so that he die, shall surely be put to death.

§6.4 <u>Matthew 5:21-22</u>   You have heard that it was said by them of old time, You shall not kill, and whosoever shall kill shall be in danger of the judgment. But I say unto you, that whosoever is angry with his brother without a cause shall be in danger of the judgment, and whosoever shall say to his brother, Raca (Empty Head), shall be in danger of the council, but whosoever shall say, you fool, shall be in danger of hell fire.

§6.5 <u>Hebrews 9:27</u>   And, as it is appointed unto men once to die, but after this the judgment.

§6.6 <u>II Corinthians 5:10</u>   For we must all appear before the judgment seat of the Messiah, that everyone may receive the things done in his body, according to that he has done, whether it be good or bad.

§6.7 Life should never be taken away except by Him who gave it. Mankind does not exist and perish like the animals. They have a soul, which is considered to be a part of Yahweh that returns to Yahweh to receive its reward or punishment in accordance with their merits and deeds done during its life on earth. Death does not terminate life, the body may die, but the spirit lives on.

Chapter 7

You shall not commit adultery

(Exodus 20:14 / Deuteronomy 5:18)

§7.1 <u>Deuteronomy 22:22</u>   If a man be found lying with a woman married to an husband, then they shall both of them die, both the man that lay with the woman, and the woman. So shall You put away evil from Israel.

§7.2 <u>Proverbs 5:15</u>   Drink waters out of your own cistern, and running waters out of your own well.

§7.3 <u>Proverbs 5:16</u>   Let your fountain be blessed and rejoice with the wife of your youth.

§7.4   <u>Proverbs 5:3-5</u>   For the lips of a strange woman drop as an honeycomb, and her mouth is smoother than oil. But her end is bitter as wormwood, sharp as a two-edged sword. Her feet go down to death her steps take hold on hell.

§7.5   <u>Proverbs 6:26-29 and 32</u>   For by means of a whorish woman a man is brought to a piece of bread, and the adulteress will hunt for the precious life. Can a man take fire in his bosom and his clothes not be burned? Can one go upon hot coals, and his feet not be burned? So he that goes in to his neighbor's wife, whosoever touches her shall not be innocent. But whoso commits adultery with a woman lacks understanding. He that does so destroys his own soul.

§7.6   <u>Matthew 5:28</u>   But I say unto you, that whosoever looks on a woman to lust after her has committed adultery with her already in his heart.

§7.7 <u>Job 31:1</u> I made a covenant with mine eyes, why then should I think upon a maid?

Chapter 8

You shall not steal.

(Exodus 20:15 / Deuteronomy 5:19)

§8.1   Deuteronomy 25:7   If a man be found
stealing any of his brethren of the
children of Israel, and makes
merchandise of him, or sells him, then
that thief shall die, and you shall put
evil away from among you. (See also
Exodus 21:16).

§8.2   Exodus 22:1   If a man shall steal an ox,
or a sheep, and kill it, or sell it, he shall
restore five oxen for an ox, and four
sheep for a sheep.

§8.3   Exodus 22:4 and 7   If the theft be
certainly found in his hand alive,

whether it be ox, or ass, or sheep, he shall restore double, let him pay double.

§8.4 <u>Leviticus 6:4</u>   He shall restore that which he took by robbery.

§8.5 <u>Proverbs 29:24</u>   Whoever is partner with a thief hates his own soul.

§8.6 <u>Ephesians 4:28</u>   Let him that stole steal no more, but rather let him labor working with his hands the thing which is good, that he may have to give to him that has need.

§8.7 It is forbidden to buy stolen goods from a thief, or a robber, or held for safekeeping anything which has apparently been stolen or acquired by robbery.

§8.8 It is not good to use anything of your neighbor's without his knowledge or to derive even the slightest benefit from a stolen article.

Chapter 9

You shall not bear false witness against your neighbor.

(Exodus 20:16 / Deuteronomy 5:20)

§9.1 <u>Proverbs 12:22</u>   Lying lips are an abomination to Yahweh.

§9.2 <u>Proverbs 14:5</u>   A faithful witness will not lie, but a false witness will utter lies.

§9.3 <u>Proverbs 19:5 and 9</u>   A false witness shall not be unpunished, and he that speaks lies shall not escape . . . shall perish.

§9.4   Exodus 23:1   You shall not raise a false report, put not your hand with the wicked to be an unrighteous witness.

§9.5   Psalm 119:104   Through Your precepts I get understanding therefore I hate every false way.

§9.6   Proverbs 6:16 and 19   Six things Yahweh hates, yea, seven are an abomination: A false witness that speaks lies, and he that sows discord among the brethren.

§9.7   Proverbs 26:28   A lying tongue hates those that are afflicted by it, and a flattering mouth works ruin.

§9.8   Revelation 21:8   But the fearful, and unbelieving, and the abominable, and murderers, and whoremongers, and sorcerers, and idolaters, and all liars, shall have their part in the lake which burns with fire and brimstone, which is the second death.

41

Chapter 10

You shall not covet.

(Exodus 20:17 / Deuteronomy 5:21)

§10.1 <u>Proverbs 3:31</u> Envy not the wicked and choose none of his ways.

§10.2 <u>Proverbs 24:1</u> Be not envious against evil men, neither desire to be with them.

§10.3 <u>Matthew 6:21</u> For where your treasure is, there will your heart be also.

§10.4 <u>Job 5:2</u>   Wrath kills the foolish man, and envy slays the silly one.

§10.5 <u>I John 2:15-16</u>   Love not the world, neither the things of the world. If any man love the world, the love of the Father is not in him. For all that is in the world, the Lust of the flesh, and the lust of the eyes, and the pride of life, is not of the Father, but is of the world.

§10.6 <u>Ephesians 5:3, and 5</u>   Fornication, and all uncleanness, or covetousness, let it not be once named among you. For this you know, that no whoremonger, nor unclean person, nor covetous man, who is an idolater, has any inheritance in the Kingdom of the Messiah and of Yahweh.

Chapter 11

You shall love your neighbor as yourself.

(Leviticus 19:18 / Romans 13:9)

§11.1 <u>Leviticus 19:13</u> You shall not defraud your neighbor, neither rob him.

§11.2 <u>Deuteronomy 15:11</u> The poor shall never cease out of the and, therefore I command you saying, You shall open your hand wide unto your brother, to your poor, and to the needy, in the land.

§11.3 <u>Matthew 5:24</u> Give to him that asks of you, and from him that would borrow from you turn not you away.

§11.4 <u>Romans 13:10</u>   Love works no ill to his neighbor; therefore love is the fulfilling of the law.

§11.5 <u>Galatians 5:14</u>   All the law is fulfilled in one word, you shall love your neighbor as yourself.   (See also: Leviticus 19:18; Matthew 19:19; Mark 12:31-33; Luke 10:25-27; Romans 13:9-10, and James 2:8-9).

§11.6 <u>Isaiah 58:6-7</u>   Is not this the fast that I have chosen? To loose the bands of wickedness, to undo the heavy burdens, and to let the oppressed go free, and that you break every yoke? Is it not to deal your bread to the hungry, and that you bring the poor that are cast out to your house? When you see the naked, that you cover him, and that you hide not yourself from your own flesh?

§11.7 <u>Matthew 25:34-36</u>   Come you blessed of my Father, inherit the Kingdom prepared for you from the foundation of the world, for I was hungered, and you gave me meat. I was thirsty and you gave me drink, I was a stranger, and you took me in, naked, and you clothed me. I was sick, and you visited me. I was in prison, and you came unto me.

§11.8 <u>Matthew 25:40</u>   And the King shall answer and say unto them, Verily I say unto you, inasmuch as you have done it unto one of the lease of these my brethren, you have done it unto me.

§11.9 <u>Zechariah 8:16</u>   Speak every man the truth to his neighbor execute the judgment of truth and peace in your gates.

§11.10 <u>Zechariah 8:17</u>   Let none of you imagine evil in your hearts against his neighbor, and love no false oath. For all these are things that I hate, says Yahweh.

§11.11 <u>Proverbs 3:28-29</u>   Say not unto your neighbor "Go and come again, and tomorrow I will give it to you", when you have it by you. Devise not evil against your neighbor, seeing he dwells securely by you.

§11.12 <u>Jeremiah 22:13</u> Woe unto him that builds his house by unrighteousness, and his chambers by wrong, that uses his neighbor's service without wages, and gives him not for his work.

§11.13 <u>Romans 5:2</u> Let every one of us please his neighbor for his good to edification (being built up).

Chapter 12

Love one another as I have loved you.

(John 13:34)

§12.1 <u>John   15:12-13</u>   This   is   my
commandment, that you love one
another, as I have loved you. Greater
love has no man than this that a man
lay down his life for his friends.

§12.2 <u>John 13:35</u>   By this shall all men
know that you are my disciples, if you
have love one to another.

§12.3 <u>I Thessalonians 4:9</u>   As touching
brotherly love, you are taught of
Yahweh to love one another.

§12.4 John 13:34   A new commandment I give unto you, that you love one another, as I have loved you, that you also love one another.

§12.5 Romans 12:9-10   Let love be without dissimulation, Abhor that which is evil, cleave to that which is good. Be kindly affectionate one to another with brotherly love, in honor preferring one another.

§12.6 I Corinthians 10:24   Let no man seek his own, but every man another's wealth.

§12.7 Romans 13:8   Owe no man anything, but to love one another, for he that loves another has fulfilled the law.

§12.8 Galatians 6:2   Bear one another's burdens, and so fulfill the law of the Messiah.

§12.9   Proverbs 10:12   Love covers all sins.

§12.10 Proverbs 17:9   He that covers a transgression seeks love.

.

§12.11 I Peter 4:8   And above all things have fervent love among yourselves, for love shall cover the multitude of sins.

§12.12 I Corinthians16:14 Let all your things be done with love.

§12.13 I John 3:14   We know that we have passed from death unto life, because we love the brethren. He that loves not his brother abides in death.

§12.14 I John 5:1-2 By this we know that we love the children of Yahweh, when we love Yahweh and keep His Commandments. This is the love of Yahweh that we keep His

Commandments, and His Commandments are not grievous.

§12.15 <u>Matthew 7:12; Luke6:31</u> Therefore all things whatsoever you would that men should do to you, do you even so to them, for this the law and the prophets.

§12.16 <u>Luke 6:30</u> Give to every man that asks of you, and of him that takes away your goods ask them not again.

§12.17 <u>Leviticus 19:34</u> But the stranger that dwells with you shall be unto you as one born among you, and You shall , love him as yourself , for you were strangers in the land of Egypt, I am Yahweh your God.

§12.18 <u>Deuteronomy 10:19</u> Love therefore the stranger, for you were strangers in the land of Egypt.

§12.19 <u>Leviticus 19:32</u>   You shall rise up before the hoary head, and honor the face of the old man, and fear Yahweh. I am the Lord.

§12.20 <u>I Timothy 5:1</u>   Rebuke not an elder but entreat him as a father.

§12.21 <u>I Timothy 5:19</u>   Against an elder receive not an accusation, but before two or three witnesses.

§12.22 <u>Exodus 22:21-22</u>   Any widow or orphan you shall not afflict. For if he cry unto me, I shall hearken unto his cry.

§12.23 <u>Proverbs 23:11</u>   Yahweh will plead their cause.

§12.24 One must speak kindly to orphans and widows, to treat them respectfully, and not to vex them even in words, because their souls are downcast and their spirits are low, even if they are wealthy.

§12.25 <u>I Timothy 5:3, and 5</u>   Honor widows that are widows indeed . . . She that is a widow indeed and desolate, trusts in Yahweh, and continues in supplications and prayers night and day.

§12.26 We must fear and revere our teachers more than our father. While our fathers have given us life in this world, the teacher prepares us for life in the World to Come.

§12.27 It is necessary to reverence and honor a man learned in the Scriptures, even if he is not advanced in years and even if he is not our teacher.

§12.28 It is also required to respect and honor a person of seventy years or over, even if he is unlearned, provided he is not an evil doer.

§12.29 <u>I Timothy 5:8</u> If any provide not for his own, and especially for those of his own house, he has denied the faith, and is worse than an infidel.

§12.30 <u>Galatians 6:9-10</u> Let us not be weary in well doing, for in due season we shall reap, if we faint not. Let us do good unto all men, especially unto them who are of the household of the faith.

Chapter 13

He is a Jew, which is one inwardly, and circumcision is that of the heart, in the spirit.

(Romans 2:28)

§13.1 <u>Philippians 3:3</u>   We are the circumcision, which worship Yahweh in the spirit.

§13.2 <u>Isaiah 65:1</u> I am sought of them that asked not for me. I am found of them that sought me not. I said, "Behold me," unto a nation that was not called by my Name.

§13.3 <u>Romans 9:24</u> Even us, whom He has called, not of the Jews only, but also of the Gentiles.

§13.4 <u>Hosea 2:23</u> And I will have mercy upon her that had not obtained mercy, and I will say to them which were not my people, you are my people, and they shall say, you are my God.

§13.5 <u>Hosea 1:10</u> And it shall come to pass, that in the place where it was said unto them, you are not my people, there it shall be said unto them, you are the sons of the living God.

§13.6 <u>Deuteronomy 10:16</u> Circumcise therefore the foreskin of your heart, and be no more stiff-necked.

§13.7 <u>Leviticus 26:41</u> If then their uncircumcised hearts be humbled.

§13.8 <u>Jeremiah 4:4</u> Circumcise yourselves to Yahweh, and take away the foreskins of your heart.

§13.9 <u>Deuteronomy 30:6</u> Yahweh your God will circumcise your heart, and the heart of your seed, to love Yahweh your God with all your heart, and with all your soul, that you may live.

§13.10 <u>Galatians 3:29</u> If you are Messiah's then are you Abraham's seed, and heirs according to the Promise.

§13.11 <u>Romans 2:28-29</u> He is not a Jew, which is one outwardly, neither is that circumcision, which is outward in the flesh. But he is a Jew, which is one inwardly, and circumcision is that of the heart, in the spirit, and not in the letter, whose praise in not of men, but of Yahweh.

§13.12 <u>Ephesians 2:14</u> For He is our peace, who has made both one, and has broken down the middle wall of partition between us.

§13.13   <u>Ephesians 2:15-16</u> To make in Himself of twain one new man, so making peace. That He might reconcile both unto Yahweh in one body by the tree having slain the enmity thereby.

Chapter 14

The life of the flesh is in the blood, and I have given it to upon the altar to make atonement for your souls for it is the blood that makes atonement for the soul.

(Leviticus 17:11)

§14.1 <u>Hebrews 9:22</u> Without the shedding of blood there is no remission of sin.

§14.2 <u>Leviticus 1:3</u> Let him offer a male without blemish. He shall offer it of his own voluntary will at the door of the Tabernacle of the Congregation before Yahweh.

§14.3 <u>Leviticus 1:4</u> And he shall put his hand upon the head of the burnt offering, and it shall be accepted for him to make atonement for him.

§14.4 <u>Leviticus 1:5</u> Aaron's sons, shall bring the blood, and sprinkle the blood round about upon the altar that is by the door of the Tabernacle.

§14.5 <u>Leviticus 1:9</u> And the priest shall burn all on the altar, to be a burnt sacrifice, an offering made by fire, of a sweet savor unto Yahweh.

§14.6 <u>Matthew 26:28</u> For this is my blood of the New Covenant, which is shed for many for the remission of sins.

§14.7 <u>Ephesians 1:7</u> In whom we have redemption through His blood, the forgiveness of sins, according to the riches of His Grace.

§14.8 <u>Joel 2:23</u> And it shall come to pass that whosoever shall call on the name of

Yahshua shall be saved. (See also Acts 2:23).

§14.9 <u>John 10:17-18</u> Therefore does my Father love me, because I lay down my life, that I might take it again. No man takes it from me but I lay it down of myself. I have power to lay it down, and I have power to take it again.

§14.10 <u>Hebrews 2:9</u> But we see Yahshua, who was made a little lower than the angels for the suffering of death, crowned with glory and honor, that He by the Grace of Yahweh should taste death for every man.

§14.11 <u>Hebrews 2:14</u> That through death He might destroy him that had the power of death, that is, the devil.

§14.12 <u>Hebrews 2:17-18</u> That He might be a merciful and faithful High Priest in things pertaining to Yahweh, to make reconciliation for the sins of the people.

§14.13 <u>Hebrews 9:12 and 28</u> Neither by the blood of goats and calves, but by His own blood He entered in once into the Holy place, having obtained eternal redemption for us. . So the Messiah was once offered to bear the sins of many, and unto them that look for Him shall - He appear the second time without sin unto salvation.

§14.14 <u>John 3:3, and 5</u> Except a man be born again, he cannot see the Kingdom of Yahweh. Except a man be born of water and of the spirit, he cannot enter into the Kingdom of Yahweh.

§14.15 <u>I Peter 1:23</u> Being born again, not of corruptible seed, but of incorruptible, by the Word of Yahweh which lives and abides forever.

§14.16 <u>I John 5:5</u> Who is he that over cometh the world, but he that believes that Yahshua is the Son of Yahweh.

§14.17 <u>Acts 2:38</u> Repent and be baptized every one of you in the name of Yahshua the Messiah for the remission of sins, and you shall receive the gift of the Holy Ghost.

Chapter 15

All the tithe of the land, whether of the seed of the land, or of the fruit of the tree, is Yahweh's. It is Holy unto Yahweh.

(Leviticus 27:30)

§15.1 <u>Deuteronomy 14:22</u> You shall truly tithe all the increase of your seed, that the field brings forth year by year.

§15.2 <u>Deuteronomy 14:23</u> The tithe of the corn, of your wine, and of your oil, and the firstlings of your herds and of the flocks, that you may learn to fear Yahweh your God always.

§15.3 <u>Deuteronomy 14:28-29</u> At the end of three years you shall bring forth all the tithe of your increase the same year, and shall lay it up within your gates.

§15.4 <u>Deuteronomy 12:6</u> And the Levite, and the stranger and the fatherless, and the widow, which are within your gates, shall come and shall eat and be satisfied; that Yahweh your God may bless you in all the work of your hand which you do.

§15.5 <u>Leviticus 27:31</u> If a man will at all redeem ought of his tithes, he shall add thereto the fifth part thereof.

§15.6 <u>Leviticus 27:32</u> Concerning the tithe of the herd, or of the flock, even whatsoever passes under the rod, the tenth shall be Holy unto Yahweh.

§15.7 <u>Numbers 18:24</u> The tithes of the children of Israel, which they offer as an heave offering unto Yahweh, I have given to the Levites to inherit. (See also Hebrews 7:5).

§15.8 Numbers 18:26   When you take of the children of Israel the tithes which I have given you from them for your inheritance, then you shall offer up a heave offering of it for Yahweh, even a tenth part of the tithe. (See also Hebrews 7:9).

§15.9 Nehemiah 10:35-36 And to bring the first-fruits of our ground and the first-fruits of all fruit of all trees, year by year, unto the house of Yahweh. Also the firstborn of our sons and of our cattle, as it is written in the law, and the firstlings of our herds and of our flocks, to bring to the house of Yahweh, unto the priests that minister in the house of our God. (See also Hebrews 7:5).

§15.10 Nehemiah 10:38 The priest, the son of Aaron shall be with the Levites when the Levites take tithes, and the Levites shall bring up the tithe of the tithes unto the house of our God. (See also Hebrews 7:9)

§15.11 <u>Malachi 3:10-12</u>   Bring all the tithes into the storehouse, that there may be meat in mine house, and prove me now herewith, saith Yahweh, Lord of Hosts, if I will not open you the windows of heaven, and pour out a blessing, that there shall not be room enough to receive it. And I will rebuke the devourer for your sakes, and he shall not destroy the fruits of your ground, neither shall your vine cast her fruit before the time in the field, saith Yahweh, Lord of Hosts. And all nations shall call you blessed, for you shall be a delightsome land, saith Yahweh.

§15.12 <u>Proverbs 3:9-10</u>   Honor Yahweh with your substance, and with the first-fruits of all your increase, so shall your barns be filled with plenty, and your presses shall burst out with new wine.

§15.13 <u>II Corinthians 9:6-7</u>   He who sows sparingly shall reap also sparingly and he who sows bountifully shall reap - also bountifully. Every man according as he purposes in his heart, so let him

give; not grudgingly, or of necessity;
for Yahweh loves a cheerful giver.

§15.14 <u>Luke 6:38</u> Give, and it shall be given
unto you, good measure, pressed
down, and shaken together, and
running over, shall men give into your
bosom. For with the same measure that
you mete withal it shall be measured to
you again.

Chapter 16

It shall be kept for the congregation of the children of Israel for a water of separation it is a purification for sin.

(Numbers 19:9)

§16.1 <u>Numbers 19:20</u>   But the man that shall be unclean, and shall not purify himself, that soul shall be cut off from among the congregation, because he has defiled the sanctuary of Yahweh. The Water of Separation has not been sprinkled upon him.   (See also John 3:5)

§16.2 <u>John 3:5</u> Except a man be born of water and the spirit, he cannot enter the Kingdom of Heaven.

§16.3 <u>Acts 2:38</u> Repent and be baptized every one of you in the name of Yahshua the Messiah for the remission of sins, and you shall receive the gift of the Holy Ghost.

§16.4 <u>Acts 16:30-33</u> Sirs, what must I do to be saved? Believe on Yahshua the Messiah, and you shall be saved and your house. And he took them the same hour of the night, and washed their stripes, and was baptized, he and all his, straightway.

§16.5 <u>Romans 6:3-4</u> Know you not that so many of us as were baptized into Yahshua the Messiah were baptized into His death? Therefore, we are buried with Him by baptism into death. As Messiah was raised up from the dead by the glory of the Father, even so we also should walk in newness of life. (See also Colossians 2:12)

§16.6 <u>Acts 6:7</u> And the word of Yahshua increased; and the number of the disciples multiplied in Jerusalem greatly, and a great number of the priests were obedient to the faith.

§16.7 <u>Acts 21:20</u> You see brother, how many thousands of Jews there are which believe; and of the Law they are all zealous of the Law.

Chapter 17

Be kind one to another, tender hearted, forgiving one another even as Yahweh for Messiah's sake has forgiven you.

(Ephesians 4:32)

§17.1 <u>Proverbs 25:21-22</u> If your enemy be hungry, give him bread to eat, and if he be thirsty give him water to drink, for you shall heap coals of fire upon his head, and Yahweh shall reward you. (See also Romans 12:20).

§17.2 <u>Proverbs 24:17-18</u> Rejoice not when your enemy falls, and let not your heart be glad when he stumbles, lest Yahweh see it, and it displease Him, and He turn away His wrath from him.

§17.3 <u>Romans 12:14</u> Bless them which persecute you, bless, and curse not.

§17.4 <u>Matthew 5:44</u> Love your enemies, bless them that curse you, do good to them that hate you, and pray for them which despitefully use you, and Persecute you. (See also Luke 6:27-31).

§17:5 <u>Matthew 6:14-15</u> If you forgive men their trespasses, your heavenly Father will also forgive you. But if you forgive not men their trespasses, neither will your Father forgive your trespasses.

§17.6 Mark 11:25 When you stand praying forgive, if you have ought against any, that your Father also which is in heaven may forgive you your trespasses.

§17.7 <u>Mark 11:26</u> If you do not forgive neither will your Father, which is in heaven forgive your trespasses.

§17.8 <u>Luke 17:3-4</u> If your brother trespass against you, rebuke him, and if he repent, forgive him. And if he trespasses against you seven times a day, and seven times a day turn again to you saying, I repent, you shall forgive him.

§17.9 <u>Colossians 3:13</u> Forbearing one another, and forgiving one another. Even as Messiah forgave you, so also do you.

§17.10 <u>I John 1:9</u> If we confess our sins, He is faithful and just to forgive us our sins and to cleanse us from all unrighteousness.

PART II

The Dietary Law

Chapter 18

You shall therefore put difference between clean beasts and unclean, and between unclean fowls and clean, and you shall not make your souls abominable by beast, or by fowl, or by any manner of living thing that creeps on the ground, which I have separated from you as unclean. And you shall be Holy unto me, for I Yahweh am Holy, and have severed you from other people, that you should be mine.

(Leviticus 20:25-26)

§18.1 <u>Leviticus 11:2</u> These are the beasts that you shall eat among all the beasts of the earth. (See also Deuteronomy 14:4).

§18.2 <u>Leviticus 11:.44-45</u> I am Yahweh your God you shall therefore sanctify yourselves, and you shall be Holy, for I am Holy. Neither shall you defile yourselves with any manner of creeping thing that creeps upon the earth. I am Yahweh that brings you up out of the land of Egypt to be your God. You shall therefore be Holy for I am Holy.

§18.3 <u>Leviticus 11:46-47</u> This is the law of the beasts, and of the fowl, and of every living creature that moves in the waters, and of every creature that creeps upon the earth, to make a difference between the unclean and the clean, and between the beast that may be eaten and the beast that may not be eaten. (See also Leviticus 11:1-23 and Deuteronomy 14:1-21).

§18.4 <u>Deuteronomy 14:2-3</u> For you are a Holy people unto Yahweh your God, and Yahweh has chosen you to be a peculiar people unto Himself, above all nations that are upon the earth. You shall not eat any abominable thing.

§18.5 <u>Deuteronomy 14:4-6</u> These are the beasts which you shall eat: The ox, the sheep, the goat, the hare, the roebuck, the fallow deer, the wild goat, the pygarg (mountain goat), the wild ox (antelope), and the chamois (mountain sheep). And every beast that parts the hoof, and cleaves the cleft into two claws, and chews the cud among the beasts, that shall you eat. (See also Leviticus 11:3).

§18.6 <u>Deuteronomy 14:9</u> These shall you eat of all that are in the waters. All that have fins and scales shall you eat.

§18.7 <u>Leviticus 11:9</u> Whatsoever has fins and scales in the waters, in the seas, and in the rivers, them shall you eat.

§18.8 <u>Deuteronomy 14:11 and 20</u> Of all clean birds you shall eat . . . of all clean fowls you may eat.

§18.9 <u>Leviticus 11:21</u> Yet these may You eat of every flying creeping thing that goes upon all fours, which have legs above their feet, to leap withal upon the earth.

§18.10 <u>Leviticus 11:22</u> Even these of them you may eat, the locust after his kind, and the bald locust after his kind, and the beetle after his kind, and the grasshopper after his kind.

Chapter 19

You shall not eat any abominable thing.

(Leviticus 11:4/Deuteronomy 14:7)

§19.1 <u>Leviticus 11:4-7</u> These shall you not eat of them that chew the cud, or of them that divide the hoof, as the camel, because he chews the cud, but divided not the hoof, he is unclean unto you. And the swine (pig), though he divide the hoof, and be cloven footed, yet he chews not the cud. He is unclean to you. [Note: Deuteronomy 14:7-8, includes the hare (rabbit)]. These are all unclean unto you. You shall not eat of their flesh, nor touch their dead carcass.

§19.2 <u>Deuteronomy 14:10</u> And whatsoever has not fins and scales you may not eat, it is unclean to you.

§19.3 <u>Leviticus 11:10-11</u>   And all that have not fins and scales in the seas, and in the rivers, of all that move in the waters, and of any living thing which is in the waters, they shall be an abomination unto you, you shall not eat of their flesh, but you shall have their carcasses in abomination.

§19.4 <u>Leviticus 11:12</u> Whatsoever has no fins or scales in waters that shall be an abomination unto you, (See also Deuteronomy 14:10) you may not eat, it is an abomination to you.

§19.5 <u>Leviticus 11:13-19</u> And these are they which you shall have in abomination among the fowls, they shall not be eaten, they are an abomination: The eagle, the ossifrage (vulture), the osprey (buzzard), after his kind. And the vulture (falcon), the glede, and the kite after his kind. And every raven after his kind, the owl, the night hawk, the cuckow, and the hawk after his kind. The little owl, the cormorant, the great owl, the swan, the pelican, the gier eagle, the stork, the heron after her kind, the lapwing, and the bat.

§19.6 <u>Deuteronomy 14:19</u>   And every creeping (swarming) thing that flies is unclean unto you. They shall not be eaten. All other flying creeping things, which have four feet shall be an abomination unto you.

§19.7 <u>Leviticus 11:24</u> Whoever touches the carcass of them shall be unclean until evening.

§19.8 <u>Leviticus 11:29</u> These also shall be unclean unto you among the creeping things that creep upon the earth, the weasel, and the mouse, and the tortoise after his kind, and the ferret, and the chameleon, and the lizard, and the snail, and the mole. These are unclean to you among all that creep. Whosoever touches them, when they be dead, shall be unclean until even.

§19.9 <u>Leviticus 11:32</u> And upon whatsoever any of them, when they are dead, doth fall, it shall be unclean, whether it be any vessel of wood, or raiment, or skin, or sack, whatsoever vessel it be, wherein any work is done, it must be put into water, and it shall be unclean until the even, so it shall be cleansed.

§19.10 <u>Leviticus 11:33</u> Every earthen vessel, where into any of them falls, whatsoever is in it shall be unclean, and you shall break it. (Leviticus 15 12, and every vessel of wood shall be rinsed in water)

§19.11 <u>Leviticus 11:35</u> Everything whereupon any part of their carcasses fall shall be unclean, whether it be oven, or ranges for pots, they shall be broken down, for they are unclean, and shall be unclean unto you.

§19.12 <u>Leviticus 11:36</u> Nevertheless, a fountain or pit, wherein there is plenty of water, shall be clean, but that which touches their carcasses shall be unclean.

§19.13 I Timothy 4:4 Every creature of Yahweh is good and nothing to be refused, if it be received with thanksgiving, for it is sanctified by the Word of Yahweh and prayer. [Note: Clean animals have been sanctified by the Word of Yahweh and are to be received with thanksgiving and prayer. However, unclean animals are not sanctified by the Word of Yahweh, and no amount of prayer can make them clean for eating. We make our souls an abomination by eating them]. (See also Leviticus 20:25-26).

§19.14 Isaiah .66:1 5, and 17 For, behold, Yahweh will come with fire, and with His chariots like a whirlwind, to render His anger with fury, and His rebuke with flames of fire they that sanctify themselves, and purify themselves in the gardens behind one tree in the midst, eating swine's flesh, and the abomination, and the mouse, shall be consumed together, saith Yahweh.

§19.15 <u>Leviticus 3:16-17</u>   All the fat is Yahweh's. It shall be a perpetual statute for your generations throughout all your dwellings, that you eat neither fat nor blood.

Chapter 20

Food Preparation

§20.1 Meat and dairy products may not be eaten or cooked together, nor is it permissible to derive any benefit from such mixed foods.

§20.2 From the dough made of one of the five species of grain (wheat, barley, spelt, rye, and oats), the Hallah portion must be separated. Immediately before separating the Hallah, the following benediction is recited:

BLESSED IS YAHWEH OUR GOD, KING OF THE UNIVERSE, WHO HAS SANCTIFIED US BY HIS COMMANDMENTS, AND HAS

COMMANDED US TO SEPARATE
THE HALLAH.

(Then dough no less than the size of an olive
is separated and burned. The custom is
to burn it in the same oven where the
bread is being baked.)

§20.3 The leaven taken from dough for
fermenting other dough, should be
removed before the Hallah has been
separated.

§20.4 Before the meat is salted it must be
thoroughly rinsed with water. The
meat should be soaked and entirely
submerged in water for half an hour.

§20.5 Frozen meat must be allowed to thaw
out before being salted.

§20.6 The meat should remain in the salt for
one hour, but in case of an emergency,
twenty-four minutes is sufficient.

§20.7 After the meat has remained in the salt for the proper length of time, the salt should be thoroughly shaken off and the meat rinsed three times.

Chapter 21

Preparation of Vessels

§21.1 Glass and metal utensils for culinary, purposes, must be immersed in water before they may be used.

§21.2 Before immersion of vessels, the following benediction is recited:

BLESSED IS YAHWEH OUR GOD, KING OF THE UNIVERSE, WHO HAS SANCTIFIED US BY HIS COMMANDMENTS, AND COMMANDED US CONCERNING THE IMMERSION OF A VESSEL.

§21.3 Wooden, Clay, and porcelain vessels need not be immersed, unless they have metal hoops.

§21.4 Only vessels used to hold food ready to be eaten without any further preparation need to be immersed.

§21.5 Before immersing the vessel, it must be thoroughly cleansed.

Chapter 22

Benedictions over the Food

§22.1 Before eating food over which a benediction has been made, we should wash both hands, and recite the benediction:

BLESSED IS YAHWEH OUR GOD, KING OF THE UNIVERSE, WHO HAS SANCTIFIED US BY HIS COMMANDMENTS AND HAS COMMANDED US CONCERNING THE WASHING OF THE HANDS.

§22.2 The time of benediction can be either before or after the meal. But in either case we should not leave the table without saying Grace.

§22.3 The benediction over the bread is recited:

BLESSED IS YAHWEH OUR GOD, KING OF THE UNIVERSE, WHO HAS BROUGHT FORTH BREAD FROM THE EARTH.

§22.4 The benediction over the wine (grape juice); is recited:

BLESSED IS YAHWEH OUR GOD, KING OF THE UNIVERSE, WHO CREATES THE FRUIT OF THE VINE.

§22.5 Each participant should drink at least four ounces of the wine or grape juice.

Chapter 23

Kosher Laws

§23.1 Kosher does not mean Biblically correct, it means that a Rabbi has deemed a certain item proper or fit.

§23.2 All food and their components are divided into four categories:

      a. Meat

      b. Dairy

      c. Parve (neutral)

      d. Non-Kosher

§23.3 Kosher means that clean animals must be slaughtered in a religiously-mandated humane way by skilled and learned Jews

§23.4 Dairy products must be derived from Kosher animals.

§23.5 Parve includes everything else that is still considered Kosher, which includes eggs, Kosher fish, and plants (fruits and vegetables). Only fish with scales and fins are Kosher. Parve products may be eaten with either meat or dairy products although fish may not be mixed with meat in a single dish.

§23.6 Non-Kosher foods include all unclean beasts, fowl, fish, and creeping things, and also as a result of food processing.

§23.7 Sabbath and holiday meals should include wine or grape juice, two loaves of bread (rolls or matzos), fish and meat.

§23.8 Work proscription (no work allowed) for Biblically-mandated festivals are generally the same as for the Sabbath.

§23.9 On the eve of fast days there is a need to eat well before sundown. On fast days the need is to wait until after sundown to consume any food or drink.

§23.10 In an institutional environment, Kosher foods can be made by:

a. Preparing it on site with proper kitchen facilities,

b. Obtaining pre-packaged meals from Kosher food venders with products having an appropriate Kosher certification symbols.

c. Obtaining fresh products through retail outlets and Kosher food purveyors

§23.11 The use of disposable plastic or paper goods is an easy, cost-effective and religiously-acceptable alternative when providing Kosher food in an institutional setting.

§23.12 The letter "K" alone printed on a food package is a generic letter and does not indicate that any reputable certifying organization has provided any oversight.

§23.13 Six of the most commonly accepted national Kosher certification agencies are:

a. The Union of Orthodox Jewish Congregations

b. The Organized Kashrus Laboratories.

c. "Star-K" Kosher Certification.

d. "Kof-K" Kosher Supervision

e. Central Rabbinical Congress.

f. K'hal Adath Jeshurun

§23.14 The letter "D' following some of these symbols signifies that the item contains dairy products and may not be used with meat products.

PART III

The Moral Law

Chapter 24

Man does not live by bread alone, but by every word that proceeds out of the mouth of Yahweh.

(Deuteronomy 8:3 / Matthew 4:4 / Luke 4:4)

§24.1 Matthew 5:3 Blessed are the poor in spirit, for theirs is the Kingdom of heaven.

§24.2 Mathew 5:4 Blessed are they that mourn, for they shall be comforted.

§24.3 Matthew 5:5 Blessed are the meek, for they shall inherit the earth.

§24.4　Matthew 5:6　Blessed are they which do hunger and thirst after righteousness, for they shall be filled.

§24.5　Matthew 5:7　Blessed are the merciful, for they shall obtain mercy.

§24.6　Matthew 5:8　Blessed are the pure in heart, for they shall see Yahweh

§24.7　Matthew 5:9　Blessed are the peacemakers, for they shall be called the children of Yahweh.

§24.8　Matthew 5:10　Blessed are they which are persecuted for righteousness sake, for their's is the Kingdom of Heaven.

§24.9　Matthew 5:11 Blessed are you, when men shall revile you, and persecute you, and say all manner of evil against you falsely, for my sake.

§24.10 <u>Matthew 5:12</u>   Rejoice and be exceedingly glad, for great is your reward in Heaven, for so persecuted they the prophets which were before you.

§24.11 <u>Matthew 5:13</u>   You are the salt of the earth, but if the salt have lost its savor, wherewith shall it be salted.

§24.12 <u>Matthew 5:14-15</u> You are the light of the world, let your light so shine before men, that they may see your good works, and glorify your Father in Heaven.

§24.13 <u>Matthew 5:25-26</u>   Agree with your adversary quickly, while in the way with him, lest he take you to the judge, and you be put in prison.

§24.14 <u>Matthew 5:32</u>   Whoever shall put away his wife, saving for the cause of fornication causes her to commit adultery, and whosoever shall marry her that is divorced commits adultery.

§24.15 <u>Matthew 6:1-4</u> When you do alms, let not your left hand know what your right had doeth, that your alms may be in secret, and your Father which sees in secret Himself shall reward you openly.

§24.16 <u>Matthew 6:5</u> When you pray, enter into your closet, and when You hast shut your door, pray to your Father which is in secret, and your Father which sees you in secret, shall reward you openly.

§24.17 <u>Matthew 6:7</u> When you pray, use not vain repetitions, as the heathen do, for they think that they shall be heard for their much speaking.

§24.18 <u>Matthew 6:17-18</u> When you fast, anoint your head and wash your face, that You appear not unto men to fast, but unto your father, which is in secret and your Father which sees in secret shall reward you openly.

§24.19 <u>Matthew 6:20-21</u> Lay up treasures in heaven, where neither moth or rust doth corrupt, and where thieves do not break through or steal, for where your treasure is there will your heart be also

§24.20 <u>Matthew 6:24</u> No man can serve two masters, for either he will hate the one, and love the other, or else he will hold to the one, and despise the other. You cannot serve Yahweh and mammon (riches).

§24.21 <u>Matthew 6:33-34</u> Seek first the Kingdom of Yahweh, and His righteousness, and all these things shall be added unto you. Take no thought for tomorrow, for the morrow shall take thought for the things of itself.

§24.22 <u>Matthew 7:1-2</u> Judge not, that you be not judged, for with what judgment you judge, you shall be judged.

§24.23 <u>Matthew 7:7</u> Ask and it shall be given you, seek, and you shall find, knock, and it shall be opened unto you.

§24.24 <u>Matthew 7:8</u> Everyone that asks receives, and he that seeks finds, and to him that knocks it shall be opened.

§24.25 <u>Matthew 7:13-14</u> Enter you in at the strait (narrow) gate, for wide is the gate, and broad is the way, that leads to destruction. Because strait (narrow) is the gate and narrow is the way, which leads unto life, and few there be that find it.

§24.26 <u>Matthew 7:16</u> Beware of false prophets, which come in sheep's clothing, but inwardly are ravening wolves. You shall know them by their fruits.

§24.27 <u>Matthew 7:21</u> Not everyone that saith unto me, Lord, Lord, shall enter the Kingdom of Heaven, but he that does the will of my Father which is in Heaven.

§24.28 <u>Matthew 10:16</u> Be you therefore wise as serpents, and harmless as doves.

§24.29 <u>Matthew 10:22</u> You shall be hated of all men for my name's sake, but he that endures to the end shall be saved.

§24.30 <u>Deuteronomy 28:1-2</u> If you shall hearken diligently unto the voice of Yahweh your God, to observe and to do all His commandments that Yahweh your God will set you on high above all nations of the earth, and all these blessings shall come on you, and overtake you.

§24.31 Deuteronomy 28:3 Blessed shall you be in the city and blessed shall you be in the field.

§24.32 Deuteronomy 28:4 Blessed shall be the fruit of your ground, and the fruit of your cattle, the increase of your kine (cattle), and the flocks of your sheep.

§24.33 Deuteronomy 28: Blessed shall be your basket and they store.

§24.34 Deuteronomy 28:6 Blessed shall you be when you come in, and blessed shall you be when you go out.

§24.35 Deuteronomy 28:7 Yahweh shall cause your enemies that rise up against you to be smitten before your face they shall come out against you one way, and flee before you seven ways.

§24.36 <u>Deuteronomy 28:8</u>   Yahweh shall command the blessing upon you in your storehouses and in all that you set your hand to do and He shall bless you in the land which Yahweh your God gives you.

§24.37 <u>Deuteronomy 28:9</u>   Yahweh shall establish you a Holy people unto Himself.

§24.38 <u>Deuteronomy 28:10</u> All the people of the earth shall see that you are called by the name of Yahweh, and they shall be afraid of you.

§24.39 <u>Deuteronomy 28:11</u> Yahweh shall make you plenteous in goods.

§24.40 <u>Deuteronomy 28:12</u>   Yahweh shall open unto you His good treasure, the heaven to give the rain unto your land in his season, and to bless all the work of your hand.

§24.41 Deuteronomy 28:13 Yahweh shall make you the head, and not the tail, and you shall be above only, and you shall not be beneath, if you hearken unto the commandments of Yahweh your God, to observe and to do them.

Chapter 25

You shall therefore obey the voice of Yahweh your God, and do His commandments and His statutes.

(Deuteronomy 27:10)

§25.1 <u>Deuteronomy 27:15</u>   Cursed be the man that makes any graven or molten image, an abomination unto Yahweh.

§25.2 <u>Deuteronomy 27:16</u>   Cursed be he that sets light (treats with contempt) by his father or his mother.

§25.3 <u>Deuteronomy 27:17</u>   Cursed be he that removes his neighbor's land mark.

§25.4 <u>Deuteronomy 27:18</u> Cursed be he that makes the blind to wander out of the way.

§25.5 <u>Deuteronomy 27:19</u> Cursed be he that perverts the judgment of the stranger, fatherless, and the widow.

§25.6 <u>Deuteronomy 27:20</u> Cursed be he that lies with his father's wife.

§25.7 <u>Deuteronomy 27:21</u> Cursed be he that lies with any manner of beast.

§25.8 <u>Deuteronomy 27:22</u> Cursed be he that lies with his sister.

§25.9 <u>Deuteronomy 27:23</u> Cursed be he that lies with his mother in law.

§25.10 <u>Deuteronomy 27:24</u> Cursed be he that smites his neighbor secretly.

§25.11 Deuteronomy 27:25   Cursed be he that takes reward to slay an innocent person.

§25.12 Deuteronomy 27:26   Cursed be he that confirms not all the words of this law to do them.

Chapter 26

Curses for Disobedience

(Deuteronomy 28:15-68)

§26.1 <u>Deuteronomy 28:15</u> It shall come to pass, if you will not hearken unto the voice of Yahweh your God, to observe and do all His Commandments and His statutes, that all these curses shall come upon you, and overtake you.

§26.2 <u>Deuteronomy 28:16</u> Cursed shall you be in the city, and cursed shall you be in the field.

§26.3 <u>Deuteronomy 28:17</u> Cursed shall be your basket and your store.

§26.4   Deuteronomy 28:18 Cursed shall be the
        fruit of your body, and the fruit of your
        land, the increase of your kine (cattle),
        and the flocks of your sheep.

§26.5   Deuteronomy 28:19 Cursed shall you be
        when you come in, and cursed shall you
        be when you go out.

§26.6   Deuteronomy 28:20   Yahweh will send
        upon you cursing, vexation, and rebuke,
        in all that you set your hand unto for to
        do. Until you be destroyed, and until
        you perish quickly, because of the
        wickedness of your doings, whereby
        you has forsaken me.

§26.7   Deuteronomy 28:21-45   Yahweh shall
        make the pestilence cleave unto you;
        shall smite you with a consumption,
        and a fever; shall make the rain of your
        land powder and dust, shall cause you
        to be smitten before your enemies; will
        smite you with the blotch of Egypt;
        shall smite you with madness;

You shall betroth a wife, and another man shall lie with her; your ox shall be slain before your eyes; they sons and your daughters shall be given unto another people; the fruit of your land and all your labors, shall a nation which you know not eat up;

Yahweh shall smite you in the knees and the legs with a sore blotch that cannot be healed, from the sole of your foot to the top of your head; You shall carry much seed out into the field, and shall gather in little. You shall plan a vineyard, but shall neither drink of the wine, nor gather the grapes, for the worms shall eat them. All your trees and fruit of your land shall the locust consume.

All these curses shall come upon you and shall pursue you, and overtake you, till you are destroyed, because you hearkened not unto the voice of Yahweh your God, to keep His Commandments and His statutes which He commanded you.

Chapter 27

Miscellaneous Laws

§27.1 <u>Ezekiel 44:23-24</u>   They (the priests) shall teach my people the difference between the Holy and profane, and cause them to discern between the unclean and the clean.   And in controversy they shall stand in judgment, and they shall judge it according to my judgments, and they shall keep my Laws and my statutes in all mine assemblies, and they shall hallow my Sabbaths.

§27.2   <u>I Corinthians 6:2-3</u>   Do you not know that the saints shall judge the world? And if the world shall be judged by you, are you unworthy to judge the smallest matters? Know you not that we shall judge angels? How much more are you worth to judge things that pertain to this life.

§27.3   Ezekiel 33:6 If the watchman see the sword come, and blow not the trumpet, and the people be not warned, if the sword come, and take any person from among them, he is taken away in his iniquity, but his blood will I require at the watchman's hand.

§27.4   Ezekiel 33:13   If he (the righteous) trust in his own righteousness, and commit iniquity, all his righteousness shall not be remembered, but for his iniquity that he has committed, he shall die for it.

§27.5   Ezekiel 33:18   When the righteous turns from his righteousness, and commits iniquity, he shall even die thereby.

§27.6   Ezekiel 33:19   But if the wicked turn from his wickedness and do that which is lawful and right, he shall live thereby.

§27.7   Deuteronomy 25:16   All that do unrighteously are an abomination unto Yahweh your God.

§27.8   Deuteronomy 24:12   If a man be poor, you shall not sleep with his pledge.

§27.9   Deuteronomy 24:14-15   You shall not oppress a hired servant that is poor and needy. You shall give him his hire neither shall the sun go down upon it, for he is poor and sets his heart upon it, lest he cry against you unto Yahweh, and it will be a sin unto you.

§27.10 Leviticus 25:35   If your brother be waxen poor, and fallen in decay with you, then you shall relieve him, yea, though he be a stranger, or a sojourner, that he may live with you.

§27.11 Exodus 22:22-24   You shall not afflict any widow, or fatherless child. If you afflict them in any wise, and they cry at unto me, I will surely hear their cry, and my wrath shall wax hot, and I will kill you with the sword, and your wives shall be widows, and your children fatherless.

§27 .12 Leviticus 19:9   You shall not wholly reap the corners of your field, neither shall you gather the gleanings of your harvest.

§27.13 Leviticus 19:10   You shall not glean your vineyard, neither shall you gather every grape of your vineyard, you shall leave them for the poor and stranger. I am Yahweh your God.

§27.14 Leviticus 19:14   You shall not curse the deaf, nor put a stumbling block before the blind, but you shall fear Yahweh your God.

§27.15 Deuteronomy 25:4   You shall not muzzle the ox when he treads out the corn.

§27.16 Deuteronomy 22:10   You shall not plow with an ox and an ass together.

§27.17 Proverbs 12:10   A righteous man regards the life of his beast.

§27:18 Exodus 23:12   On the seventh day you shall rest, that your ox and your ass may rest.

§27.19 Exodus 23:4-5   If you meet your enemy's ox or his ass going astray, you shall surely bring it back to him again. If you see the ass of him that hates you lying under his burden, and would forbear to help him, you shall surely help with him.

§27.20 Deuteronomy 22:4   You shall not see your brother's ass or his ox fall down by the way, and hide yourself from them, you shall surely help him to lift them up again.

§27.21 Deuteronomy 22:6-7   If a bird's nest chance to be before you in the way in any tree, or on the ground, whether they be young ones, or eggs, and the dam sitting upon the young, or upon the eggs, you shall not take the dame with the young. But you shall in any wise let the dam go, and take the young to you, that it may be well with you, and that you may prolong your days.

§27.22 Deuteronomy 24:17   You shall not pervert the judgment of the stranger, nor the fatherless, not take a widow's raiment to pledge.

§27.23 <u>Deuteronomy 25:1</u>   You shall justify the righteous, and condemn the wicked.

§27.24 <u>Leviticus 19:15</u>   You shall do no unrighteousness in judgment, you shall not respect the person of the poor, nor honor the person of the mighty, but in righteousness shall you judge your neighbor.

§27.25 <u>Deuteronomy 16:19-20</u>   You shall not west judgment, You shall not respect persons, neither take a gift, for a gift doth blind the eyes of the wise, and pervert the words of the righteous. That which is altogether just shall you follow.

§27.26 <u>Psalm 82:3-4</u>   Defend the poor and fatherless, do justice to the afflicted and needy, deliver the poor and needy. Rid them out of the hand of the wicked.

§27.27 <u>Proverbs 17:23</u>   A wicked man takes a gift out of the bosom to pervert the ways of judgment.

§27.28 <u>Deuteronomy 23:27</u>   There shall be no whore of the daughters of Israel, or a sodomite of the sons of Israel.

§27.29 <u>Leviticus 19:29</u>   Do not prostitute your daughter, to cause her to be a whore, lest the land fall to whoredom, and the land become full of wickedness.

§27.30 <u>Proverbs 23:27</u>   A whore is a deep ditch, and a strange woman is a narrow pit.

§27.31 <u>Leviticus 18:16</u>   You shall not uncover the nakedness of your brother's wife, it is your brother's nakedness.

§27.32 <u>Leviticus 18:17</u>   You shall not uncover the nakedness of a woman and her daughter, it is wickedness.

§27.33 <u>Leviticus 18:20</u>   You shall not lie carnally with your neighbor's wife, to defile yourself with her.

§27.34 <u>Leviticus 18:22</u>   You shall not lie with mankind, as with womankind, it is abomination.

§27.35 <u>Leviticus 20:13</u>   If a man also lie with mankind, as he lies with a woman, both of them have committed an abomination. They shall surely be put to death. Their blood shall be upon them.

§27.36 <u>Romans 1:32</u>   Who knowing the judgment of Yahweh, that they which commit such things are worthy of death, not only do the same, but have pleasure in them that do them.

§27.37　Deuteronomy 23:18　You shall not bring the hire of a whore, or the price of a dog, into the house of Yahweh your Yahweh for any vow, for even both these are abomination unto Yahweh your God.

§27.38　Leviticus 18:23　Neither shall you lie with any beast to defile yourself therewith, neither shall any woman stand before a beast to lie down thereto, it is confusion.

§27.39　Leviticus 20:25-16　If a man lie with a beast, he shall surely be put to death, and you shall slay the beast. If a woman approach unto any beast, and lie down thereto, you shall kill the woman, and the beast.

§27.40　Exodus 22:19　Whoever lies with a beast shall surely be put to death.

§27.41　Deuteronomy 22:25　If a man find a betrothed damsel in the field, and the man force her, and lie with her, then the man only that lay with her shall die.

§27.42 Deuteronomy 22:5   The woman shall not wear that which pertains unto a man neither shall a man put on a woman's garment, for all that do so are an abomination unto Yahweh your God.

§27.43 Leviticus 19:26   You shall not eat anything with the blood, neither shall you use enchantment, nor observe times.

§27.44 Leviticus 19:28   You shall not make any cuttings in your flesh for the dead, nor print any marks upon you.

§27.45 Exodus 22:18   You shall not suffer a witch to live.

§27.46 Leviticus19:31   Regard not them that have familiar spirits, neither seek after wizards to be defiled by them.

§27.47 Leviticus 20:27   A man also or woman that has a familiar spirit, or that is a wizard, shall surely be put to death. They shall stone them with stones. Their blood shall be upon them.

§27.48 Deuteronomy 18:10-12   There shall not be found among you any one that makes his son or his daughter to pass through the fire, or that uses divination, or an observer of times, or an enchanter, or a witch, or a charmer, or a consulter with familiar spirits, or a wizard, or a necromancer. For all that do these things are an abomination unto Yahweh.

§27.49 Deuteronomy 24:16   The fathers shall not be put to death for the children, neither shall the children be put to death for the fathers every man shall be put to death for his own sin.

§27.50 <u>Deuteronomy 25:3</u>   Forty stripes he may give him, and not exceed.

§27.51 <u>Deuteronomy 21:22-23</u>   If a man has committed a sin worthy of death, and he is to be put to death, and you hang him on a tree, his body shall not remain all night upon the tree, but you shall in any wise bury him that day, (for he that is hanged is accursed of Yahweh), that the land be not defiled.

§27.52 <u>Deuteronomy 25:13</u>   You shall not have in your bag divers weights, a great and a small.

§27.53 <u>Deuteronomy 23:20</u>   Unto a stranger you may lend upon a usury, but unto your brother You shall not lend upon usury, that Yahweh your God may bless you in all that you set your hand to in the land whither you go to possess it.

§27.54 <u>Leviticus 19:11</u>   You shall not steal, neither deal falsely, neither lie one to another.

§27.55 <u>Leviticus 19:16</u>   You shall not go up and down as a talebearer among your people, neither shall you stand against the blood of your neighbor.

§27.56 <u>Leviticus 19:17</u>   You shall not hate your brother in your heart.

§27.57 <u>Leviticus 19:18</u>   You shall not avenge, nor bear any grudge against the children of your people.

§27.58 <u>Ecclesiastes 5:1</u>   Keep they foot when you go to the house of Yahweh, and be more ready to hear than to give the sacrifice of fools, for they consider not that they do evil.

§27.59 <u>Ecclesiastes 5:4</u>   When you vow a vow unto Yahweh, defer not to pay it, for He has no pleasure in fools, pay that which you have vowed.

§27.60 <u>Ecclesiastes 9:9</u>   Live joyfully with the wife whom you love all the days of the life of your vanity.

§27.61 <u>Ecclesiastes 9:10</u>   Whatever your hand finds to do, do it with all your might for there is no work, nor device, nor knowledge, nor wisdom, in the grave whither you go.

§27.62 <u>Colossians 3:17 and 23</u>   Whatever you do in word or in deed, do all in the name of Yahshua, giving thanks to Yahweh, the Father by Him. And whatever you do, do it heartily, as to Yahweh, and not unto men.

Chapter 28

It is expedient for you that I go away, for if I go not away, the Comforter will not come unto you, but if I depart, I will send Him unto you.

And when He is come, He will reprove the world of sin, and of righteousness, and of judgment. Of sin, because they believe not on me, of righteousness, because I go to my Father, of Judgment, because the prince of this world is judged. (John 1 6:7-11)

And it shall come to pass afterward, that I will pour out my Spirit upon all flesh, and your sons and your daughters shall prophesy, your old men shall dream dreams and your young men shall see visions. (Joel 2:38 / Acts 2:17)

§28.1 <u>Acts 1:5 and 8</u>   John truly baptized with water, but you shall be baptized with the Holy Ghost not many days hence. You shall receive power after that the Holy Ghost is come upon you, and you shall be witnesses unto me both in Jerusalem, and in all Judaea, and in Samaria, and unto the uttermost part of the earth.

§28.2 <u>Romans .12:6-8</u>   Having then gifts differing according to the Grace that is given to us, whether prophecy, let us prophesy according to the proportion of faith. Or ministry let us wait on our ministering, or he that teaches, on teaching, or he that exhorts, on exhortation, he that shows mercy, with cheerfulness.

§28.3 <u>I Corinthians 12:4-11</u>   Now there are diversities of gifts, but the same Spirit, and there are differences of administrations, but the same Lord. And there are diversities of operations, but it is the same Yahweh which works all in all. But the manifestation of the

Spirit is given to every man to profit withal.

For to one is given by the Spirit the Word of Wisdom, to another the Word of Knowledge by the same Spirit, to another Faith by the same Spirit, to another the Gifts of Healing by the same Spirit, to another the Working of Miracles, to another Prophecy, to another Discerning of Spirits, to another Divers Kinds of Tongues, to another the Interpretation of Tongues. But all these work that one and the selfsame Spirit, dividing to every man severally as He will.

§28.4 I Corinthians 14:39   Covet to prophesy, and forbid not to speak with tongues.

§28.5 Galatians 5:16 Walk in the spirit, and you shall not fulfill the lust of the flesh.

§28.6 <u>Galatians 5:22-25</u>   The Fruit of the Spirit is Love, Joy, Peace, Longsuffering, Gentleness, Goodness, Faith, Meekness, Temperance. Against such there is no law. And they that are Christ's have crucified the flesh with the affections and lusts. If we live in the Spirit, let us also walk in the Spirit.

§28.7 <u>Galatians 5:19-21</u>   The works of the flesh are manifest, which are: Adultery, Fornication, Uncleanness, Lasciviousness, Idolatry, Witchcraft, Hatred, Variance, Emulations, Wrath, Strife, Seditions, Heresies, Envyings, Murders, Drunkenness, Revellings, and such like. They which do such things shall not inherit the Kingdom of Yahweh.

§28.8 <u>Revelation 21:8</u>   But the fearful, and unbelieving, and the abominable, and murderers, and whoremongers, and sorceress, and idolaters, and all liars, shall have their part in the lake which burns with fire and brimstone, which is the second death.

§28.9 <u>John 14:26</u>   The Helper, the Holy Spirit, whom the Father will send in my name, He will teach you all things, and - bring to your remembrance all things that I said to you.

§28.10 <u>Romans 8:13</u>   If by the Spirit you put to death the deeds of the body, you will live.

§28.11 <u>John 16:13</u>   When He, the Spirit of Truth has come, He will guide you into all truth.

§28.12 <u>Ephesians 4:11</u>   He gave some Apostles, and some Prophets, and some Evangelists, and some Pastors and Teachers, for the perfecting of the saints, for the work of the ministry, for the edifying of the body of the Messiah.

§28.13 It is the sacred duty of every Believer to have implicit faith in Yahweh, and to look only to Him in time of trouble, distress and sickness. Salvation and healing can only come through repentance, baptism in the name of Yahshua, and a conscientious turning to Yahweh to do those things that are pleasing to our Father in Heaven.

Chapter 29

I have taken the Levites from among the children of Israel instead of all the firstborn that opens the matrix among the children or Israel. Therefore the Levites shall be mine, because all the firstborn are mine.

For on the day that I smote all the firstborn in the land of Egypt I hallowed unto me all the firstborn in Israel, both man and beast, mine shall they be. I am Yahweh.

(Numbers 3:12-13; Exodus 34:19)

§29.1   Exodus 29:29   The firstborn of your sons shall you give to me.

§29.2 <u>Numbers 18:15</u> The firstborn of man shall you surely redeem.

§29.3 Redemption is made when the father brings his firstborn son to the priest and gives him the price of redemption. (102 grams of pure silver)

§29.3 The priest accepts the money and gives the son back to the father. Kiddush (communion) is served with the appropriate blessings and a feast is usually prepared in honor of the redemption of the firstborn.

Chapter 30

When you shall come into the land, and shall have planted all manner of trees for food, and then you shall count the fruit thereof as uncircumcised. Three years shall it be as uncircumcised to you. It shall not be eaten.

But in the fourth year all the fruit thereof shall be Holy to praise Yahweh withal. In the fifth year shall you eat of the fruit thereof, that it may yield unto you the increase thereof. I am Yahweh your God.

(Leviticus 19:23-25)

§30.1   The enjoyment of the fruit, seeds, and skins of all kinds of trees are entirely forbidden as orlah. (During the first three years)

§30.2 The fruits of the fourth year's growth is called Nata rebai, (the growth of the fourth year), and it must be redeemed. To redeem the fruit of the fourth year take the fruit after it is fully ripe, and with a silver coin, or the smallest coin in circulation and say: "With this I redeem the fruit of the fourth year." Then destroy the coin or the produce and throw it into a river.

§30.3 If one has planted a seed, or a branch, or has transplanted a tree, he must consider the fruit as orlah. However, if one graft a branch upon a tree, the law of orlah does not apply.

§30.4 The prohibition of grafting dissimilar trees is implied in Leviticus 19:19: "You shall not sow your field with mingled seed." (See also Deuteronomy 22:9). It is therefore forbidden to graft the branch of one variety of trees upon another, such as the branch of an apple tree upon a citrus bearing tree.

§30.5   It is permissible to transplant a branch of a grafted tree.

§30.6 <u>Leviticus 19:19</u>   You shall not let your cattle gender with a diverse kind.

§30.7 It is forbidden to cross-breed cattle, beasts or fowl with a diverse kind.

§30.8 <u>Deuteronomy 22:10</u> You shall not plow with an ox and an ass together.

Chapter 31

These words shall be in your heart, and you shall teach them diligently unto your children, and shall talk of them when you sit in your house, and when you walk by the way, and when you lie down, and when you rise up.

(Deuteronomy 6:6-7 and 11:19)

§31.1 It is the duty of the father to train his children in the practice of all the precepts. It is also required of the father to protect his children from any forbidden acts. If words are of no avail, the father should chastise him with a rod.

But he should never strike his child mercilessly. The father should take special care to teach his children to tell no lies, and to speak the truth at all times.

§31.2 As soon as a child understands the significance of the Sabbath service, it become the child's duty to hear the Kiddush (Blessings of the wine and the bread), and the Havdalah (Closing of the - Sabbath). It is important that the child be trained to behave in the service with awe and reverence.

§31.3 If a child steals anything, he should be forced to return the stolen article if it is still intact.

§31.4 A parent should not threaten a child with future punishment. If he sees him misbehave, he should either punish him at once, or ignore it

§31.5 <u>Deuteronomy 4:9</u>   Every father is required to teach Scriptures to his children, and to his grandchildren, as it is said: "You shall make them known to your children and to your children's children."

§31.6 A teacher should not punish the students like an enemy, with malice and cruelty, nor with a whip or a stick, but with a light strap.

§31.7 It is forbidden to rob a minor of anything he has found, especially something that was given to him as a gift.

§31.8 As soon as a child begins to talk he should be taught the Scriptures little by little until he begins school. At which time Yahweh fearing teachers are employed to train the child to be Yahweh fearing from his youth.

§31.9 Children should not be given to the heathen to be instructed in reading and writing, or to be taught a trade, for it is to be feared that they will follow in his footsteps.

§31.10 Ephesians 5:25-26; 28   Husbands love your wives even as the Messiah loved the Church, and gave Himself for it . . . So ought men to love their wives as their own bodies. He that loves his wife loves himself. (See also I Peter 3:1, 7)

§31.11 Ephesians 5:22-23   Wives submit yourselves unto your own husbands, as unto Yahweh. The husband is the head of the wife, even as the Messiah is the head of the Church. (See also Colossians 3:18 and I Peter 3:5-6)

§31.12 Colossians 3:20   Children obey your parents in all things, for this is pleasing unto Yahweh.

§31.13 Colossians 3:21   Fathers, provoke not your children to anger, lest they be discouraged.

§31.14 I Peter 3:7   Yahweh has endowed marriage with a touch of holiness. Women have equality with the men in all things, and were created as helpers in raising families and in service to Yahweh, as it is said: "As being heirs together of the grace of life, that your prayers be not hindered."

§31.15 <u>II Corinthians 6:14-15</u>   Be not unequally yoked together with unbelievers, for what fellowship has righteousness with unrighteousness? And what communion has light with darkness? And what concord has Messiah with Belief? Or, what part has he that believeth with an infidel?

Chapter 32

*Evening, Morning, and at Noon, will I pray
and cry aloud, and Yahweh shall hear my voice.*

(Psalm 55:17)

§32.1 Daniel 6:10 He (Daniel) kneeled upon his knees three times a day, and prayed, and gave thanks before Yahweh, as he did aforetime.

§32.2 The Morning (Shacharit) prayer is prayed immediately upon rising.

§32.3 The Afternoon (Minchah) prayer is prayed at any time from 3:30 pm to sunset.

§32.4 The Evening (Maariv) prayer is prayed after darkness.

§32.5 Immediately upon rising one should give thanks to Yahweh, for His mercies are new every morning.

§32.6 Before entering into prayer and Bible study everyone should wash their faces and hands, and brush their teeth in preparation for worshipping Yahweh.

§32.7 <u>Numbers 15:38-40</u> Speak unto the children of Israel and bid them that make them fringes in the borders of their garments throughout their generations, and that they put upon the fringe of the borders a ribbon of blue.

It shall be to you for a fringe, that you may look upon it and remember all the commandments of Yahweh, and do them; and that you seek not after your own hurt and your own eyes, after which you use to go whoring, that you may remember and do all my commandments and be Holy unto your God. (See also Deuteronomy 22:12)

§32.8 <u>Deuteronomy 11:18</u>   Therefore shall you lay up these my words in your heart and in your soul, and bind them for a sign upon your hand, that they may be as frontlets between your eyes.

§32.9 <u>Proverbs 7:3</u>   Bind them upon your fingers write them upon the table of your heart.

§32.10 Tefillin (Phylacteries) are put on after the Tallit (Prayer Shawl). The precept which is observed regularly takes precedence over a precept which is not observed regularly. The precept of the fringed garment (Tallit) is to be performed daily, including Sabbaths and festivals, while the precept of the Tefillin is to be observed on weekdays only.

§32.11 <u>Deuteronomy 6:9</u>   You shall write them upon the doorpost of your house and upon your gates.

§32.12 <u>Proverbs 3:3</u>   Let not mercy and truth forsake you, bind them about your neck and write them upon the table of your heart. (See also Proverbs 6:21)

§32.13 <u>Proverbs 6:21</u>   The Mezuzah must be affixed to the right hand side as one enters, and attached within the upper third of the doorpost.

§32.14 We place the parchment containing the Shema so that the word Shema is on the top, and place it in the receptacle, and fasten it with nails to the doorpost diagonally, having the top line containing the first word Shema towards the house, and the last line towards the outside. We must fasten it with nails at the top and at the bottom.

§32.15 Because the purpose of the Mezuzah is to remember His Name, Yahweh, and we should kiss the Mezuzah upon leaving the house and upon entering it. Upon leaving the house and placing our hand on the Mezuzah, we say: "Yahweh is my Keeper. Yahweh is my shade upon my right hand. Yahweh shall preserve my going out and my coming in, from this time forth and forever more."

§32.16 Deuteronomy 6:4-5   Hear, O Israel, Yahweh is our God, Yahweh is one, you shall love Yahweh your God with all your heart, with all your soul, and with all your might.

§32.17 Mark 12:29 Yahshua answered him, the first of all the commandments is Hear, O Israel, Yahweh is our God, you shall love Yahweh your God with all your heart, with all your soul, with all your mind, and with all your strength." (See also Matthew 22:37-38).

§32.18 It is customary to recite aloud the verse:

"Shema Yisrael, Adonai Eloheinu, Adonai Echad."

(Hear O Israel, Yahweh is our God, Yahweh is one)

[Place the right hand upon our eyes. After saying **echad**, we pause a little and then say]:

"Baruch shem kvod malchuto l'olam vaed."

(Blessed is His Name and His glorious Kingdom forever and ever.)

§32.19 The Shema is said two times daily, once in the morning upon rising, before the Morning Prayer, and again at night during the Evening Prayer.

PART IV

The Feasts of Yahweh

Chapter 33

These are the Feasts of Yahweh, even Holy Convocations, which you shall proclaim in their seasons.

(Leviticus 23)

§33.1 **SABBATH** [Shabbat] <u>Leviticus 23:3</u>
Six days shall work be done, but the seventh day is the Sabbath of rest, an Holy convocation, you shall do no work therein, it is the Sabbath of Yahweh in all your dwellings.

§33.2 **NEW MOON** [Rosh Chodesh] <u>Isaiah 66:23</u>   From one New Moon to another, and from one Sabbath to another shall all flesh come to worship before me, saith Yahweh.   (See also Numbers 10:10)

§33.3 **PASSOVER** [Eve of Pesach] <u>Leviticus 23:5</u> On the fourteenth day of the first month (Nisan) at even is Yahweh's Passover.

§33.4   **UNLEAVENED   BREAD** [Pesach] <u>Leviticus 23:6-8</u>   On the fifteenth day of the same month (Nisan), is the Feast of Unleavened Bread unto Yahweh, seven days you must eat unleavened bread. In the first day you shall have a Holy convocation, you shall do no servile (laborious) work therein. In the seventh day is a Holy convocation, you shall do no servile (laborious) work therein.

§33.5 **FIRSTFRUITS** [Sefirah 1] <u>Leviticus 23:9-14</u>   Shall bring a sheaf of the First-fruits of your harvest unto the priest, and he shall wave the sheaf before Yahweh, to be accepted for you, on the morrow after the Sabbath (Nisan 16), the priest shall wave it.

§33.6 **PENTECOST** [Shavuot] <u>Leviticus 23:15-21</u> On the morrow after the Sabbath, from the day that you brought the sheaf of the wave offering (Nisan 16), seven Sabbaths shall you number fifty days, (Sivan 6) and you shall offer a new meat offering unto Yahweh.

You shall - bring out of your habitations two wave loaves of two tenth deals, they shall be fine flour, they shall be baked with leaven, these are the First-fruits unto Yahweh. And you shall proclaim on the selfsame day (Sivan 6), that it may be a Holy convocation unto you, you shall do no servile (laborious) work therein. It shall be a statute forever in all your dwellings throughout your generations.

§33.7   **TRUMPETS**   [Rosh Hashanah] <u>Leviticus 23:23-25</u> In the seventh month (Tishrei), in the first day of the month, shall you have a Sabbath, a memorial of blowing of trumpets, a Holy convocation. You shall do no servile (laborious) work therein.

§33.8 **DAY OF ATONEMENT** [Yom Kippur] Leviticus 23:27-32 Also in the tenth day of this seventh month (Tishrei), there shall be a day of atonement, it shall be a Holy convocation unto you, and you shall afflict your souls. You shall do no work in that same day, for it is a day of atonement, to make atonement for you before Yahweh your God.

You shall do no manner of work. It shall be a statute forever throughout your generations in all your dwellings. It shall be a Sabbath of rest, and you shall afflict your souls, in the ninth day of the month (Tishrei) at even, from even unto even, shall you celebrate (observe) your Sabbath.

§33.9 **TABERNACLES** [Sukkoth] Leviticus 23:34-36 On the fifteenth day of this seventh month (Tishrei), shall be the Feast of Tabernacles for seven days unto Yahweh. On the first day will be a Holy convocation, you shall do no servile (laborious) work therein. On the eighth day shall be a Holy convocation unto you. It shall be a solemn assembly, and you shall do no servile (laborious) work therein.

§33.10 **LIGHTS AND DEDICATION** - [Chanukah] A festival of dedication held in the months of Kislev and Tevet, to be held for eight days in commemoration of the eight days the cruse of oil burned in the Temple. (Kislev 25 - Tevet 2). In John 10:22-23, it is recorded that Yahshua walked in Solomon's porch at the time of the Feast of Dedication.

§33.11 **PURIM** Esther 10:17-28 A Festival of Deliverance observed for two days on the fourteenth and fifteenth days of the month of Adar. A commemoration of Yahweh's deliverance of His children from their enemies, and that these days should be remembered and kept throughout every generation.

§33.12 <u>Leviticus 23:37-38</u> These are the Feasts of Yahweh which you shall proclaim to be Holy Convocations. This is in addition to the Sabbaths, your gifts, your vows, and all your freewill offerings which you give unto Yahweh.

§32.13 <u>Isaiah 58:13</u> It is our duty to honor all festivals and to take delight in them, just as we are to honor and take delight in the Sabbath.

§33.14 Anything forbidden on a Sabbath, is also forbidden on a festival.

§33.15 The Sabbath Closing [Havdalah] service should be conducted on Saturday evening.

§33.16 The New Moon [Rosh Chodesh] festival is a minor day of atonement. Women customarily do not have to work on Rosh Chodesh, even though work is permitted for others.

Ray Looker
(1940 -   )

Biography

Ray Looker is a disciple of Yahshua the Messiah, an apostle of the Messianic Jewish faith and has been a Professor of Theology. Ray is committed to preparing the Church for the coming of the Messiah.

Ray spent 14 years in the U.S. Army as a Senior-Ranking Non-Commissioned Officer. His military assignments took him to Greenland, Germany, Norway and Vietnam. He served in seven major campaigns in Vietnam, and has spent over 30 years as a Missionary and Professor in Europe, China and the inner-cities of America. With graduate degrees in Law Ray worked as a Law Clerk in a Public Defender's Office and with a District Court Judge while doing post-graduate work for a Doctor of Theology Degree.

His post-Doctorate research in Educational and Motivational Psychology allowed him to be a Program Manager in an epidemiological study of mental illness for the Department of Health and Mental Retardation for the State. He later served as a Director of Compliance enforcing a Federal Court Order on a maximum security prison for the criminally insane, a Justice of the Peace, a Notary Public and as an Auxiliary Police Officer in the State of New York.

Ray ran for the House of Delegates and as a Magistrate with the idea that government 'servants' were to be held accountable to the people for their actions. In addition Ray has also served as Pastor in a Christian Church, and as Messianic Rabbi in a Messianic Jewish Congregation. He has also ministered on both radio and television and has been a Baritone Soloist in various churches when asked to do so.

When the Messiah comes all men will be commanded to observe the Commandments of Yahweh, i.e., the Feasts of Yahweh, His Sabbaths, the New Moons, and the Dietary Laws of the written TORAH. Ray's work and ministry is to prepare and to teach Believers the importance of keeping Yahweh's laws and commandments in accordance with His wishes and desires for us. It might be noted that not one so-called Christian Holiday or Sabbath will be observed in the Messianic Era and Kingdom of our Lord when He comes.

To raise up the 'Tabernacle of David' in preparation for the coming of the Messiah the Church must rebuild and restore Christianity upon the bedrock foundation of the Apostles and Prophets, which is the written TORAH.

Ray's first book began his journey in the Messiah Jewish faith. His many books on Messianic Judaism are a testimony of the dedication of his life to preparing the way for the coming of the Messiah. As he is able, he intends to make these books available on the internet for worldwide access to everyone everywhere.

Printed in Great Britain
by Amazon